Men's Mi
Changing the World through
Teams and Teamwork

Dr. Brad Stewart

Teams and Teamwork

Making disciples incorporates visioning, harvesting, and building in men after conversion. This is not an easy task. Fortunately, Christ provided an example for the church by training His men. At the end of His earthly ministry, He commanded them to go make disciples (Matthew 28:18-20). The need was great then; the need is great today. Teams and Teamwork is a set of tools to help accomplish the great commission in the local church setting. At the heart of a team is training and executing the ministry.

Dr. Brad Stewart

Table of Contents

Introduction

Men's Ministry Teams and Teamwork

A few years back I was leading a Bible study with three men. To stimulate their thinking, I asked this question: "If you had three months to live, what would you do with your life?" The first individual to speak was single. He said, "I would give away all my possessions and use the money in my bank account to fly to the deepest jungle in Africa to share the gospel with an unreached people group." The second man was married and had a family. He said, "I would do two things. First, I would ensure my home is in order and my immediate family taken care of. Then, I would sit down and list all my family members who were not saved and create a plan to share the gospel with each one of them." The third man, who was married, said "I would move my mother-in-law into my home." Stunned by his answer, I asked "Why would you do that?" He replied, "Because that would be the longest three months of my life."

Granted, this story brings a chuckle. But there is a truth to the question and wisdom in the answers. Suppose you had three years to live, what would you do with your remaining time? Jesus faced the same question. He knew His time on earth was limited. So, what did He do? To find the answer to that question, we need to take a look at the Gospel of John.

In John 1, we find John the Baptist giving the first real testimony of whom Jesus is. The next day, two of His disciples decided to follow Jesus. Seeing them follow Him, Jesus asked them, "What do you want?" They replied by asking, "Where are you staying?" Jesus begins His ministry with a few simple but powerful words, "Come and you will see."

Andrew went to Simon his brother and claimed to have found the Messiah. He then brought him to Jesus. The next day Jesus found Phillip and said to him, "Follow me." Phillip then found Nathaniel and told him about Jesus. Nathaniel reacted with disbelief. Phillip's answer to Nathaniel is a classic case of mentoring and discipleship. He said, "Come and see."

In the beginning Jesus surrounded Himself with men. A few months later he prays all-night to select twelve men to be with Him to do ministry together. He knew that ministry flows out of men in strong relationships with one another. When it came time to send the disciples out to do the work of the ministry, He sent them out in groups of two and gave them specific training instructions for each mission (Luke 9:1-6; 10:1-17).

In the book of Acts we see the apostle Paul undertake three missionary journeys (Acts 13:1-4; 15:36-41; 20:4). In each journey he traveled and worked with a small group of men. Whenever he went into a city to establish a church, the first thing he did was build a ministry team that would carry on after he departed. Toward the end of several New Testament books we see a list of men and women who worked with Paul to establish new churches and build existing ones (Romans 16:3-15; Ephesians 6:21; Colossians 4:7-17)

While the principles for ministry in these Scriptural chapters are numerous, I want to point out the importance of finding like-minded men who are seeking truth and desire to make an impact in the world.

AB Bruce in his classic work provides this comment on the early ministry of Jesus,

> "That these calls were given with conscious reference to an ulterior end, even the apostleship, appears from the remarkable terms in which the earliest of them was expressed. "Follow Me," said Jesus to the fishermen of Bethsaida, "and I will make you fishers of men." These words (whose originality stamps them as a genuine saying of Jesus) show that the great Founder of the faith desired not only to have disciples, but to have about Him men whom He might train to make disciples of others: to cast the net of divine truth into the sea of the world, and to land on the shores of the divine kingdom a great multitude of believing souls. Both from His words and from His actions we can see that He attached supreme importance to that part of His work which consisted in training the twelve. In the intercessory prayer,[2.8] e.g., He speaks of the training He had given these men as if it had been the principal part of His own earthly ministry. And such, in one sense, it really was. The careful, painstaking education of the disciples secured that the Teacher's influence on the world should be permanent; that His kingdom should be founded on the rock of deep and indestructible convictions in the minds of the few, not on the shifting sands of superficial evanescent impressions on the minds of the many. Regarding that kingdom, as our Lord Himself has taught us in one of His parables to do,[2.9] as a thing introduced into the world like a seed cast into the ground and left to grow according to natural laws, we may say that, but for the twelve, the doctrine, the works, and the image of Jesus might have perished from human remembrance, nothing remaining but a vague mythical tradition, of no historical value, and of little practical influence."

Done right, and done well, teaming and training men in the principles and practices of Jesus, should influence others and help your church transform the culture and country in which you live, worship, and serve the Lord.

Q - How many men do you have that are committed to men's ministry?

Q - Who are they?

Part I – Foundations

Starting a Men's Ministry Team

An effective ministry needs to be based on a team approach rather than one individual. While one man may have the initial heart, vision, and passion for this ministry, he must develop a team of men around him to successfully change men's lives and achieve the ministry mission. A team allows more men to be involved, use their talents and spiritual gifts, encourage one another, and to accomplish more. Here are eight suggested steps for starting a men's ministry team.

Work from a Biblical Basis

Men's ministry flows from the great commission which Christ gave His men after the resurrection (Matthew 28:18-20). In His final instruction He provided two main points for going and making disciples of all nations:

> ⟨ baptize them in the name of the Father and of the Son and of the Holy Spirit
> ⟨ teach them to obey everything I have commanded you

Unfortunately, too many churches have abandoned Christ's model of leading by example for a more academic process. Men learn more and follow closer to a living example. Living as an intentional follower of Christ was never intended to be one man imparting knowledge to another. It was intended to be one man helping another walk with God and learn to reproduce life in others. The focus of godly men's ministry is to bring men together and build life into each other through life-on-life discipleship.

⟨ Baptizing Men

Baptism is a religious sacrament marked by the symbolic application of water to the head or immersion of the body into water and resulting in admission of the recipient into the community of Christians. Baptism signifies spiritual cleansing and rebirth. There are numerous examples of baptism in the New Testament (Matthew 3:16, Act_2:38-39, Acts 2:41; 8:12-16; 8:36-38; 9:18; 10:47-48; 16:15-33; 19:3-5; 1Cor. 1:13-16; 15:29; 1Pet. 3:21).

⟨ Teaching Them to Obey Christ's Commandments

Christ spent three years imparting His imperatives to His men. He expected them to obey His word and to help others understand what it means to obey His word. Today men are struggling with family, finances, work, sexuality, drugs, and alcohol. If this was not bad enough some studies show that most men over the age of thirty-five do not have a friend they can call or ask for help. An effective men's ministry should help provide solutions to all of these issues by teaching men to obey the commandments of Christ.

Life-to-life discipleship training helps men focus on areas that are specific to the unique struggles men face. The kind of training that makes men into mature disciples is the kind that helps men with obedience to the Scriptures. There are a lot of great tools to help local churches make disciples. For a list of tools and job aids visit Kingdom Warrior's tool site at www.kingdomwarrior.net/MMTools.htm.

Form the Foundation

1. *Pray, pray, and pray some more.* Develop a list of men in your church who you would like to ask to pray with you. Ask them if they would like to meet and pray for men and the men's ministry (Luke 6:12-13; Matthew 18:19-20; 9:36-39). Pray that God would bring the right man for the right position as based on his gifts, talents, and availability.

2. *Secure the pastors approval.* Most pastors would like to know what is going on in their church even if they do not have time to be active in every type of ministry. Some pastors will make themselves available for men's ministry while others may feel burdened by one more thing they have to take care of. Don't give up on gaining an active support from your pastor. If he has a lot of concerns, start out small and build from there. Be willing to labor for the kingdom.

3. *Fish for men.* Make contacts through evangelism, Bible studies, prayer meetings, worship, conferences, cell groups, and fellowship meetings. Share your passion for men's ministry and love for God's Word. Look for men who respond with a kindred spirit (Mark 3:13).

4. *Develop a broad base of relationships.* Get to know all the men in your small groups and meet with as many as possible in one-on-one. Ministry happens best through existing relationships. Half of Christ's first band of men contained three sets of brothers.

5. *Seek men with different gifts.* It is very natural for a leader to surround himself with men that look, act, and think as he does. Men that we want to become our friends. This can create a big hole in a team's effectiveness. A leader of men needs to surround himself with other men who complement his giftedness. Consider the following motivational gifts based on Romans 12: Prophecy, Giving/Sharing, Service, Administration, Teaching, Mercy/Helps, and Exhortation.

Select the Men

6. *Prayerfully select your team.* Identify three to five men with the following qualities:

   ☐ A commitment to pray for the men in your church. If a man is unwilling to commit to faithfully pray, he will not be faithful in other areas of ministry (Luke 16:10).

☐ A heart for ministry to men. How much does this individual like being around the men and seeing them grow in their personal and spiritual lives?

☐ A godly character. Men's ministry is driven by men of character. The apostle Paul gives his young pastor protégé a list of qualifications for selecting elders. Most of them had to do with a man's character. Although the leadership team is not the churches elder board, the team members should have the potential to some day serve as voting elders.

☐ A hunger to be a disciple and to disciple others. Your men should be willing to live as intentional followers of Jesus Christ and be committed to helping others live a lifetime of discipleship, or at least to submit themselves to learning the process.

☐ A life that allows sufficient time to become involved. No matter how gifted or brilliant a man may appear if he is not available to commit, it will cause more problems than blessings.

☐ A good chemistry with other men. Does this man work well with other men or for that matter other women? Some men have a difficult time shifting from being the leader of his home and work life to an environment that thrives on working with team mates.

☐ A blessing from your pastor. Be sure to inform your pastor before you ask a new man to take a position of leadership.

Write their names below.

7. *Meet with each man one-on-one.* The best way for a leader to recruit a new man to his team is to meet with him one-on-one. Start out by letting him know you have been praying about his involvement in men's ministry and that you feel it is time to talk about a certain area. Then share the vision and mission statement for your men's ministry. Give him the big picture of where you see the team going over the next few years. After explaining the vision and mission, tell him where you see him being involved.

a. *Give him a job description.* In a one-on-one meeting share with this man a specific job description for where you would like him to help you. For a set of high level examples see appendix A. Having something in writing makes the offer much clearer than a verbal invitation. Here are some additional considerations for a good job description:

> (1. Do's of his ministry responsibility
> (2. Approximate time it will take
> (3. Who they report to
> (4. Length of service
> (5. Resources available to them
> (6. Qualifications of the job

> Allow the man time to digest the contents and ask any questions for clarification

b. *Ask for a commitment.* Wrap up the conversation by asking the prospective leader to pray over this opportunity and if he's married, to talk to his wife about it before making a commitment. Give him a definite time frame for when he needs to have a response. Usually a week or two is plenty of time.

8. *Plan the size of your team.* If there are two or more of you already laboring as a men's ministry leadership team, than take some time to decide how many men you want on your team and who should talk to whom. If a team leader is just staring out, limit the team to three to five men. Start small and grow the team.

Q 1 – How many men do you have in your church?

Q 2 – What are the roles and jobs associated with running a men's ministry?

Q 3 – What is the maximum size you think the men's ministry team should be?

Principles of Teamwork

Teams in Scripture

God often uses a team to fulfill His purposes in the world through a group of men. In most cases He starts out effecting one man's life by calling him to a divine objective and giving him promises to guarantee the success. Rarely, does God start and end with just one man. Instead, He brings other men onto the scene and gives them the same divine objective or similar promises, which lead them to band together to pursue a common vision and mission.

The concept of teamwork runs throughout the Old and New Testaments. Abraham, Isaac, and Jacob all lived a nomadic life with men, women, and children working together to build and protect the family units. Moses, David, Solomon, and Nehemiah are great examples of leaders who focused on completing a kingdom type of mission and staffing a strong military. Jesus and Paul illustrate the forces of spiritual warfare for them and the men in their teams. The stories differ but the need to work with others is consistent in God's realm. Several specific examples stand out:

Abraham

When Abram heard that his relative had been taken captive, he called out the 318 trained men born in his household and went in pursuit as far as Dan. [15] During the night Abram divided his men to attack them and he routed them, pursuing them as far as Hobah, north of Damascus (Genesis 14:14-15).

David

Saul also went to his home in Gibeah, accompanied by valiant men whose hearts God had touched (1 Samuel 10:26).

All those who were in distress or in debt or discontented gathered around him, and he became their leader. About four hundred men were with him. So David and his men, about six hundred in number, left Keilah and kept moving from place to place. When Saul was told that David had escaped from Keilah, he did not go there (1 Samuel 22:2; 23:13.).

This is the classic list of David's Mighty Men and several of their key exploits (1 Samuel 23:8-39).

Sons of Izrahiah

The son of Uzzi: Izrahiah. The sons of Izrahiah: Michael, Obadiah, Joel and Isshiah. All five of them were chiefs. According to their family genealogy, they had 36,000 men ready for battle, for they had many wives and children. The relatives who were fighting men belonging to all the clans of Issachar, as listed in their genealogy, were 87,000 in all (1 Chronicles 7:3-4).

King Uzziah

Uzziah had a well-trained army, ready to go out by divisions according to their numbers as mustered by Jeiel the secretary and Maaseiah the officer under the direction of Hananiah, one of the royal officials. The total number of family leaders over the fighting men was 2,600. Under their command was an army of 307,500 men trained for war, a powerful force to support the king against his enemies. Uzziah provided shields, spears, helmets, coats of armor, bows and slingstones for the entire army. In Jerusalem he made machines designed by skillful men for use on the towers and on the corner defenses to shoot arrows and hurl large stones. His fame spread far and wide, for he was greatly helped until he became powerful (2 Chronicles 26:11-15).

Nehemiah

I went to Jerusalem, and after staying there three days I set out during the night with a few men. I had not told anyone what my God had put in my heart to do for Jerusalem. There were no mounts with me except the one I was riding on (Nehemiah 2:11-12).

Then I said to them, "You see the trouble we are in: Jerusalem lies in ruins, and its gates have been burned with fire. Come, let us rebuild the wall of Jerusalem, and we will no longer be in disgrace." I also told them about the gracious hand of my God upon me and what the king had said to me. They replied, "Let us start rebuilding." So they began this good work (Nehemiah 2:17-18).

So we rebuilt the wall till all of it reached half its height, for the people worked with all their heart (Nehemiah 4:6).

Jesus

One of those days Jesus went out to a mountainside to pray, and spent the night praying to God. When morning came, he called his disciples to him and chose twelve of them, whom he also designated apostles: Simon (whom he named Peter), his brother Andrew, James, John, Philip, Bartholomew, Matthew, Thomas, James son of Alphaeus, Simon who was called the Zealot, Judas son of James, and Judas Iscariot, who became a traitor. (Luke 6:12-16).

Jesus left there and went to his hometown, accompanied by his disciples. When the Sabbath came, he began to teach in the synagogue, and many who heard him were amazed (Mark 6:1-2).

Peter

Then Peter invited the men into the house to be his guests. The next day Peter started out with them, and some of the brothers from Joppa went along (Acts 10:23).

Paul

While they were worshiping the Lord and fasting, the Holy Spirit said, "Set apart for me Barnabas and Saul for the work to which I have called them. So after they had fasted and prayed, they placed hands on them and sent them off. The two of them, sent on their way by the Holy Spirit, went down to Seleucia and sailed from there to Cyprus (Acts 13:2-3).

Later in their ministry Paul said to Barnabas, "Let us go back and visit the brothers in all the towns where we preached the word of the Lord and see how they are doing." (Acts 13:36).

During the night Paul had a vision of a man of Macedonia standing and begging him, "Come over to Macedonia and help us." After Paul had seen the vision, we got ready at once to leave for Macedonia, concluding that God had called us to preach the gospel to them (Acts 16:9-10).

He was accompanied by Sopater son of Pyrrhus from Berea, Aristarchus and Secundus from Thessalonica, Gaius from Derbe, Timothy also, and Tychicus and Trophimus from the province of Asia (Acts 20:4)

Spiritual Enemies

The Pharisees and Sadducees came up, and testing Jesus, they asked Him to show them a sign from heaven (Matthew 16:1).

Now Judas, who betrayed him, knew the place, because Jesus had often met there with his disciples. So Judas came to the grove, guiding a detachment of soldiers and some officials from the chief priests and Pharisees. They were carrying torches, lanterns and weapons (John 18:2-3).

Conclusion

An effective team with a great leader lives to serve God and obey his Lord's divine calling. However, before answering a call from God, all great leaders learn to be great followers. If a man wants to lead, first he must learn to follow. God calls men who know how to follow Him.

Teams build God's kingdom by doing the work and winning the battles. Church pastors and men's ministry leaders must learn how to harness the power of building teams and fostering godly teamwork so others experience real transformation. The world, the flesh, and the devil work overtime to hinder kingdom ministry. In fact, every inch gained for the kingdom of God is contested by the enemy. If the church is going to impact the world, it must learn how to harness the power of building teams and fostering godly teamwork.

Q – Which Biblical examples stimulate your desire to build a godly men's ministry team?

Q – Why?

Team Definitions

According to Webster's Concise Dictionary, a team is a group of people working or playing together as a unit. A teammate is a fellow player or co-laborer on the team. Teamwork is work done by a team or unity of action as by the players or the teammates.[i] A group is a number of associated persons regarded as a unit. Teams require a leader while groups can take shape and form without a recognized organizer.

The model of a team in men's ministry includes at least five key elements:
- A common objective
- An accepted leader
- Agreement on methods and activities
- A strong sense of loyalty among the members
- A certain division of labor within the team members

The concept of teamwork has been a matter of concern to organizations and groups of people throughout history. In recent years, interest by leaders to get as much out of their teams as possible has fostered all sorts of experiments and testing of new methodologies. The world wants to maximize the effort produced by its work force so it can accomplish more work in the marketplace and thereby gain or maintain its economic welfare. Christian organizations should expend effort at maximizing its work as well. The primary focus of a men's ministry is to make disciples who produce lasting fruit and make an eternal impact in the harvest fields of the earth.

There are five key areas of interest for a men's ministry leader as he seeks to build an effective and efficient disciple making men's ministry team:

- Establish team roles and functions of team personnel
- Focus on a clear purpose as a ministry to and through men
- Build the team on godly character, competence, and chemistry
- Train them in ministry, mission, and manhood
- Motivate the team to higher levels of achievement

Each area should facilitate a process for building stronger male relationships. Throughout these areas, it is critical to build deeper interaction.

Roles and Functions

Teams are groups of people. All groups of people banding together have a need for direction, motivation, and guidance. Christian men, who want to make a difference in their community, require them as well. Leadership, teamwork, and partnering serve to create a team. If a ministry applies the principles for each area, it is more likely to be effective in achieving the overall mission purpose. Creating a solid team will achieve more than merely creating followers. Jesus and His small band of men transformed their society and changed the course of history.

Leaders/Champions

Leaders provide:

- Direction: They focus team activities and behaviors on desired common outcomes
- Motivation: They encourage appropriate team effort to accomplish desired outcomes
- Guidance: They provide information that improves the ability of a team to accomplish the desired outcomes
- Service: They serve people in an effort to achieve desired outcomes

Men's Ministry leaders (Champions) operate using two basic strategies:

- Use what exists and make things work to the best possible scenario by:
    - Giving direction through clear goals and specific objectives
    - Motivating men through recognition, rewards, and affirmation
    - Guiding men through use of performance feedback
    - Demonstrating strategy behaviors
    - Setting clear, measurable objectives
    - Asking men to serve on a team
    - Asking men to come to church
    - Meeting performance standards
    - Establishing procedures and systems to guide and support the ministry
    - Dealing with existing systems in a practical way
    - Getting things done
    - Making use of knowledge and experience
    - Taking action when needed

- Alter what exists to improve or create something new by:
    - Giving direction through vision and values
    - Motivating through setting expectations
    - Modeling new behaviors
    - Communicating high expectations

- Living up to potential
- Establishing principles to guide priorities and decision making
- Looking for opportunities to improve
- Getting ready for the future
- Taking note of new and differing perspectives
- Knowing where the ministry is going
- Communicating a vision for the future

Experienced leaders use a combination of these areas in the execution of their ministries.

Team Members

Men's Ministry team members are to:

\ Demonstrate support by:
- Giving cheerfully to the Church in time, talents, and treasures
- Assisting others to see that ministry events are done with effectiveness and efficiency
- Conforming behavior to the truth of God's Word

\ Practice trust by:
- Relying only on Jesus Christ for salvation
- Demonstrating respect for pastors and ministry leaders
- Keeping his word and commitments
- Operating without hidden agendas

\ Share participation by:
- Reaching out to those in need and providing for their welfare
- Contributing ideas and making men's ministry suggestions
- Involving other men as much as possible

Pastors

Pastors have a dual role. In addition to providing all the functions of a shepherd, they also partner with ministry leaders and other church ministries.

\ Pastors help church ministries by:
- Maintaining a spirit of openness so ministry team members and ministry leaders can openly share opinions, ideas, and information
- Demonstrating respect for others so that all ideas are considered fairly, and so that differences between ministries do not become sources of conflict or suspicion
- Ensuring all ministries act responsibly and contribute fully to the work of church ministry
- Ensuring each ministry contributes to the overall mission of the church

Pastors help grow men's ministries by:
- Giving their men and the men's ministry champion enthusiastic support and planned time for vision, council, and encouragement.
- Assisting when appropriate. All pastors have limited time and availability. Men's ministry leaders need to be sensitive to this.
- Getting involved wherever possible. This can be as little as making occasional appearances or leading an actual program or event. Studies show that the more involved the senior pastor is the stronger men's ministry grows.
- Modeling Jesus as the senior man and disciple maker. Men rarely follow women and children. They need godly male role models who demonstrate from the front line. This is by far one of the most powerful ways to grow men's ministry. Each pastor has his own style. Some prefer one-on-one, while others work best in small groups of three to six men. The process and end result is more important than the program.

To implement an effective disciple-making ministry requires both the support and involvement of the senior pastor. At first, support and involvement may seem like synonyms. They are not. Support can be offered from a distance. Involvement requires the pastor to be up close and personal. Mark 3:13-15 says, Jesus went up on a mountainside and called to him those he wanted, and they came to him. He appointed twelve-designating them apostles-that they might be *with him* and that he might *send them* out to preach and to have authority to drive out demons.

Jesus was *with his disciples*. That's more than support; that's involvement. So how did it work out? After Jesus *returned* to heaven, Acts 4:13 tells us how religious leaders responded to the courage of Peter and John: When they saw the courage of Peter and John and realized that they were unschooled, ordinary men, they were astonished and they took note that these men had been with Jesus. The biblical model for discipling men is to be *with them*, not merely support an effort to disciple them.

For champions and team members

Q – Which strategies do you apply in your current role as a men's ministry leader?

Q – Which strategies should you learn to develop?

For Pastors

Q - What is the difference between support and involvement?

Q - If you are the senior pastor, how can you be involved like Jesus was involved?

Team Leadership

The need for strong male leadership runs throughout the Old and New Testaments. Whenever God's raises up a champion, he usually starts out with a vision and then builds a team to accomplish a specific goal or task. To gain the most from a team, the men's ministry champion should apply sound principles of leadership.

Provide Direction Not Dictatorship – Men need leadership and direction not dictatorship and domination. Early on the disciples were more concerned about having a position of power and influence than making disciples or serving others. Jesus knowing the early condition of their spiritual life told them, "You know that those who are regarded as rulers of the Gentiles lord it over them, and their high officials exercise authority over them. Not so with you. Instead, whoever wants to become great among you must be your servant, and whoever wants to be first must be slave of all" (Mark 10:43-44). Giving men sound biblical directions helps build maturity as they learn and grow.

Allow Collaboration and Discussion – Adult men often require buy-in when it comes to moving forward in men's ministry. The best way to gain buy-in is by allowing the team to participate in the discussion and decision making process. Some scholars believe Paul operated this way. Paul, Silas, and Timothy worked together in ministry to the Thessalonians. Paul writes, *"We sent* Timothy, who is our brother and God's fellow worker in spreading the gospel of Christ, to strengthen and encourage you in your faith, so that no one would be unsettled by these trials. For this reason, when I could stand it no longer, *I sent* to find out about your faith. I was afraid that in some way the tempter might have tempted you and our efforts might have been useless (1 Thessalonians 3:2,5). No one doubts that Paul made the final decisions for his team, however, it was evidently preceded by a group discussion.

Illustrate a Sacrificial Servant – Jesus is the ultimate example of a sacrificial servant. His words were backed up by His life. "For even the Son of Man did not come to be served, but to serve, and to give his life as a ransom for many." (Mark 10:45). The kind of leader Jesus calls into service sacrifices for the welfare of his men. In addition, he needs to be the kind of man who will lay down his life for his friends (John 15:3). The team leader is a humble man who views the servant leader example of Christ as the highest ideal. In the Old Testament, God spoke directly to Moses and Aaron providing clear instructions about priestly duties.

Focus on the Mission – Today's fast paced life is filled with activity and motion. Without a clear objective, men lose focus and live in a motion of activity. A team leader routinely reminds the team of the unit's mission and goals as they serve Christ. Even good godly men tend to get sidetracked and need to have their objectives consistently reiterated and clarified.

Accomplish the Objective – A good team leader knows what is required to accomplish the team's objectives. If they need guidance, motivation, support, resources, or encouragement the team lead makes sure the team is equipped and getting the job done.

Live by Faith – A leader lives by faith as he keeps the team focused on the vision and mission of his organization. He must know he is on the right track and headed in the right direction. In the face of adverse circumstances, he must communicate his faith to the men on the team. Hezekiah when faced by an army led by wicked leaders who mocked his relationship with God and ridiculed his ability, connected with the prophet Isaiah and both men together called out to God (2 Chronicles 32:13-20).

Take Appropriate Action – The effective team leader will be a man of action. The man who tries to eliminate every bit of chance, reconcile every pro and con, or shrink back from acting against an advisor's counsel is weak and should not be in a position of leadership. If a leader fails in accomplishing an objective, it should be failing forward.

Stay Focused on the Work – God's man knows the power of determination. Early in the gospel of John Jesus remarks, "My food is to do the will of Him who sent Me and to accomplish His work." (John 4:34). Later towards the end of His life, He mentions work again, "I glorified You on the earth, having accomplished the work which You have given Me to do." (John 17:4). In between He worked to train the twelve and prepare them to labor in the harvest of people's souls. Kingdom men for kingdom work. The ideal leader works to accomplish the ministry and does not allow distractions to sidetrack the team's efforts in building the kingdom of God. He serves by demonstrating his own efforts as well as helping His men to maintain the team's primary objective.

Value Different Gifts and Abilities – Men have different gifts, abilities, strengths, and weaknesses. A good leader values his men and their actual as well as potential contributions to the team. A team should be a reflection of the body and contain gifts as well as parts that complement one another. If a team leader attracts men with similar gifts and interests, the team will have a weakness that sooner or later develops because all the parts are not in place.

Foster Good Morale – Moral can make or break a team filled with good men. Keeping the moral high is a critical factor in moving the team forward and keeping momentum flowing. When men are depressed or discouraged they tend to slow down. Some war experts think keeping the moral high is the greatest single factor in a successful war. High morale can be very motivating. High motivation can improve performance.

Keep Informed – Communication between the leader and his team and the team members to one another is a critical factor in accomplishing the work of a ministry. Some leaders use traditional means for communication while others are more adept at applying newer technologies such as text messaging. The important point here is to establish routine forms of communication so the team knows what is happening, progress being made, victories won, and needs being expressed.

While it is important to have a men's ministry champion, it is critical to have a leadership team in place to share the work and continue with equipping men for works of service. A men's leadership team is the heart of an effective men's ministry in your church as they pray, direct, and administer the entire men's ministry.

Q – Which sound principles of leadership are you good at applying?

Q – Which ones do you need to start applying or make improvements?

Advantages and Disadvantages

There are distinct advantages and disadvantages when ministries operate using teams to accomplish their ministry objectives.

Advantages

- *Strength in Numbers* – "Two are better than one, because they have a good return for their work: If one falls down, his friend can help him up. But pity the man who falls and has no one to help him up! Also, if two lie down together, they will keep warm. But how can one keep warm alone? Though one may be overpowered, two can defend themselves. A cord of three strands is not quickly broken (Ecclesiastes 4:9-12).

- *Balance and Cross Training* – A team of men has complementary abilities and varying depths of spirituality with the Lord. No one man has every spiritual gift or every talent he needs to accomplish the wide aspects of ministry to and through a group of men. Each member of a team is strengthened and developed by all the other members (1 Corinthians 12:14).

- *Planning and Coordination* – Men benefit by sharing ideas with each other, whether it be strategic plans of where and how to minister or more tactical plans of methods and means. Godly leaders have strong teams where they can share an idea with the team, let them attack it, probe it, and offer suggestions. When the discussion is complete the whole team is ready to participate on a planned action.

- *Protection and Encouragement* – Men banding together in loyalty to Christ and His Word provide mutual protection against the world and its attractions in the use of time and money. They protect one-another against doctrinal errors and worldly temptations. They challenge one another to maintain the disciplines of a godly man: quiet time, prayer, scripture memory, Bible study, evangelism, follow-up and developing proper relationships.

\ *Synergy and Power* – There is power in teamwork and synergy with combined effort. Two men working together are not one plus one but two squared; three men teamed together are not one plus one plus one but three raised to the third power. Team effort multiplies the individual thrust, provides the impact of numerical strength, and has the advantage of pressing into useful service Christians who are too timid to witness alone. (Leviticus 26:8; Philippians 1:27-28; Genesis 11:6; 1 Corinthians 12:21).

\ *Rapid Ministry Ramp Up* – A band of men who know where they are going attract other men who want to get going. When a man tries to start a ministry on his own, it may take him two years before he has a group of men who demonstrate life as a committed follower of Christ. If a leader starts with a team he immediately has a show case example.

\ *Vision versus Person* – A team tends to recruit to a vision rather than to an individual personality. This provides stability especially when the leader or leaders change unexpectedly. It also provides protection from the possibility of a leader propagating his weaknesses, becoming a dictator, or building a private kingdom.

\ *Learning Atmosphere* – Operating based on a team creates a better atmosphere for promoting the basics of a Christian man's life. It is well known that people take on the character of the group. You become like the people you spend time with (1 Corinthians 15:33).

\ *Experience and Training* – Leadership training and experience advance in a team context in which there are opportunities to lead and to follow, to plan and to coordinate. In addition, leaders are able to observe other leaders and team members who may become future leaders.

\ *Balance and Burnout* – A team disperses the load and takes some of the burden off the leader. This keeps men from getting burned out and produces equipped men for future works of ministry. A sense of useful service helps team members to continue laboring after their agreed tour of duty.

Disadvantages

\ *Thwart Individual Initiative* – Although local churches want to raise up men who can work with others, they also strive to develop men who can "stand in the gap" and carry responsibility even when they are alone. Somewhere along the line churches have to give men the opportunity to demonstrate what they can do on their own (Acts 6:3-8; 8:5-40). Some men who have been leaders, or who are natural leaders, may retrogress when forced into too limited of a team effort. This is especially true for small units of highly skilled leaders working in close proximity to one another.

\ *Inflexibility* – Some teams who have been training in one context have trouble fitting into another team, particularly if the philosophies or methods of operation of the two teams vary from their original team structure and training. Most teams do not consider the possibility that the training, methodology, and objectives for a team do not adequately prepare men for team members or supporting the objectives of other ministries.

\ *Exclusiveness* – Some teams develop a tendency toward exclusiveness and narrowness that is exaggerated by the team experience. Team members may become isolated from the total Christian heritage simply because the team appears to be a self-contained unit. A local team could replace church community life.

\ *Loyalty* – Teams rightly require a high degree of inner loyalty but this may create an inability to relate properly to other Christians or Christian organizations. Some men may lose the spirit of kingdom service.

\ *Diminish Man-to-Man Training* – There may be too much reliance on group training. Often in a group, training is geared to the lowest common denominator to accommodate the weaker members. Or the opposite may occur: the team effort may be pitched to such a high level that individual members falter without getting the personal attention that they need. Or the opposite may occur: the team effort may be pitched to such a high level that individual members falter without getting the personal attention that they need.

\ *Narcissism* – The team may become almost an end in itself. Reliance on the team may weaken dependence on God. Worse, the team may give the glory for what is accomplished to the team, or the team method, rather than on God (Isaiah 42:8). In this way the team may breed carnality.

\ *Group Pressure* – Within teams of men sometimes the qualities seen in a team member may be the result of group pressure rather than a genuine work of the Holy Spirit.

Q- Which advantage advantages do you see as the most influential for your church?

Q – How are they working as advantages for your current team?

Q - Which disadvantage may impact your team?

Q – What actions can you take to minimize the negative impact?

Building a Men's Ministry Team

With a few men committed to being together to form a men's ministry team, you are now ready to build the ministry. Over the course of the first year or two, it is important for the men to develop as a team which facilitates teamwork. They must begin the process of ministering together.

Teams develop as men commit to being a part of the men's ministry team. The men's ministry team must have a clear vision and mission statement to help it stay on course and to accomplish the ministry goals. Most men long for an opportunity to be a part of something bigger than themselves. If they are going to sacrifice their time with family and career, invest emotional energy, and physical resources, they want to know it's worth the time, effort, and cost. To maintain moving forward, leaders need to routinely keep the vision, mission, and goals clearly in front of the team.

If you do not already have a vision and mission statement, you need to develop them. There is a saying, "Aim at nothing and you will hit it every time." When it comes to men's ministry, having a focused direction is important. A purpose statement provides direction and forms the basis for all of ministry activities, goals, and guiding principles.

Some leaders write an end state statement that is similar to missions and vision. This can provide added guidance to the team members without a team leader. It also helps the leader begin with the end in mind.

Mission, Vision, and Guiding Principles

Vision is the biblical mandate for ministry. It is the over-arching reason for doing ministry. The vision statement is usually the broader term and serves as the ultimate ministry fulfillment. Examples:
  - Helping men find their way (Steve Farrar)
  - Serving the Lord at home, at work, and in the Church (Joshua's Men)
  - Forcefully advancing the Kingdom of Heaven through the local church (Kingdom Warrior)

Mission helps bring into view some of the specifics of what an organization believes God has called them to do. The mission statement should compel the organizations core leadership team and excite the men in the organizations ministry. In other words, it should motivate.

Examples:
  - Deepen a man's personal walk with God, Develop a man's brotherhood with other men, and Disciple a man's life for works of service (Joshua's Men)

- Through the brotherhood of Christ, we strive to help men serve God by using their time, talents, and treasures in an effort to transform their homes, their communities, and their churches for the glory of God. Kingdom Warrior accomplishes this mission by providing excellent men's ministry conferences, workshops, seminars, resources, coaching, and training services to help churches implement an ongoing ministry to and through men (Kingdom Warrior).

Guiding Principles are a set of statements that provide personal or group rules of conduct and management. Examples:
- Cultivate a male friendly environment
- Provide opportunities for men to interact
- Teach practical application of the Bible
- Disciple men as intentional followers of Jesus Christ
- Equip men for works of ministry

End State:
- Each team member acts according to Scripture when he leads in his home, work, job, or church.

Together these form a set of purpose statements. Having a clear purpose statement is critical to keeping a men's ministry focused and carrying out the ministry. Without focus, a ministry can exist but never accomplish something significant toward building the kingdom of God. Building the kingdom of God is accomplished by training men to labor in the harvest fields of men's souls. Jesus worked to train His men to fulfill the great commission.

Q - What is your vision statement?

Q – What is your mission statement?

Q – What are your guiding principles?

Q – What is your end state?

Schedule Masculine Activities

Masculine activities are a necessary part in gathering men together. Most men will attend something if they are invited, have some similar interest, or consider it of value. Here are four areas to consider in developing a strategy and scheduling a tailored men's event.

Social – Fun activities to invite Christians and non-Christians to attend
- Sports (football, baseball, basketball, golf, soccer, hockey
- Wilderness (fishing, fly fishing, hunting, hiking, camping)
- Business (Kiwanas, elections, fund raisers)
- Dining (Coffee stand, pizza, bar and grill, grilling meat)

Situational – Periodic events increasing relationships with God and men
- Monthly men's breakfast
- Annual district men's retreat
- Annual Iron Sharpens Iron or similar event
- Men's worship or rally events

Seminar – Equipping or training events with a specific focus
- Relationships (marriage, parenthood, family)
- Spiritual skills (God's will, spiritual gifts, prayer, mentoring)
- Knowledge skills (computer, vehicle repair, carpentry)
- Apologetic or evangelism seminars

Spiritual – Small group where growth has increased accountability
- Discipleship cell
- Sermon cell for men only
- Application Bible study
- Accountability cell

Build the team through joint activities: men's breakfasts, prayer meetings, Bible studies, evangelism, work projects, recreation, fellowship, worship, cell groups, and conferences. Give them plenty of opportunities to exercise their gifts and perform their assigned duties. Use each event as an opportunity to meet new men and grow the team. Pair up key men so they are meeting with other men for mutual accountability, encouragement, and growth. Focus all activities and events so they fulfill the mission, vision, and guiding principles of a Christ centered men's ministry. Involve the pastor or pastors in as many activities and ministries as time will allow. NOTE: If you are having problems getting your pastor's support or involvement, see Appendix D.

Q - Which set of activities are most appealing to you and your men?

Q - Which set of activities are least appealing to you and your men?

Plan for the Long Haul

Most solid ministries to and through men are built over a three to five-year period. Take for example the life of Jesus. Even He took three years to start and complete His ministry. You need to take a long range view to starting and running a quality men's ministry. Below is a recommended four-year vision for a startup local church men's ministry. It is only a recommendation. Each church has its own unique culture and most important its own unique men. Use this tool as a guideline for your plans.

1st Year

Get to know the men in your church. Look for men who have a heart for men's ministry. Assemble your leadership team and spend the year becoming for one another what you want the men of your church to be. Establish the model within your leadership team. During this year, do all your preparation work. Things like developing your prayer team, surveying the men of your church, writing a purpose statement that includes the vision and mission. Get your pastor's input and support.

2nd Year

Begin to develop an identity within the church. Branding is an excellent way to market your men's ministry. You want the men who attend your church to know a ministry to men exists. Consider a logo as part of your branding. You may want to add to your leadership team and kick off one or two areas of ministry: monthly men's breakfast and an annual conference.

3rd Year

Start to expand the ministry. Be sure to include small groups if you have not done so in year 2. Pick one new area of ministry and start to plan on how you will implement. Make it a goal for you and the leadership to identify a new ministry each year. Before beginning a new ministry offering, have a leader who is willing to be the point man. This leader should have the experience and skills necessary to develop a team of people to work with him, know the ministry purpose, and have a strategy in place to implement the new ministry. During this year, your executive leadership team continues to provide training for existing leaders and new leaders for the ministry. All your men's events and ministries should support your purpose statement. If you do not sense God leading you to add to your existing ministry that is OK but be sure to evaluate and identify areas for improving your existing battle plan.

4ᵗʰ Year and Continuing

Continue to move forward and fill in any empty spots. Consider planning a leadership summit once a ministry year. This will work best if it is at the end of your ministry year but in time to plan for next year. Evaluate each aspect of your current ministry. Identify where it is unbalanced or needs improvements. Make plans to balance the load or improve the standards. Evaluate if your leadership team is functioning properly or if it needs to be realigned with how the ministry has grown. Expect eventually that some men on the leadership team will move or switch ministries within the church. Plan for attrition by ensuring each leader works on mentoring someone else on the team. When you meet with them individually, ask them who is being prepared to take his position if he moves on. Paul had his Timothy. Timothy taught faithful men who were told to teach others (2 Timothy 2:2). By training replacements, you prepare new leaders.

Establish Your Ministry Milestones

Here is a basic guide to help you put a strategy into place using the information you recorded in the evaluation sections. Locate a yearly calendar for establishing deadline dates.

Measurable Goals for Your Battle Plan – Year 1	Deadline	Deadline
1. Survey the men to determine their interests and needs		1 m
2. Identify your men's ministry leadership team		2 m
3. Develop your mission, vision, and set of guiding principles		3 m
4. Develop a prayer ministry		3 m
5. Create communication tools: cards, emails, web site, newsletter…		6 m
6. Select an overall theme for your next ministry year		8 m
7. Develop a pastoral prayer ministry		8 m
8. Hold an in-house, first class entry point type of event		10-12m

Table 1 - Year 1 Suggested Milestones

Measurable Goals for Your Battle Plan – Year 2	Deadline
1. Establish your name and ministry logo	
2. Offer first special entry point for men on the periphery	
4. Offer second special entry point for men who frequently attend the church	
5. Develop the first phase of weekly small groups for men	
6. Identify your men's small group leaders	
7. Train your small group leaders in the dynamics for building men only groups	
8.	
9.	
10.	

Table 2 - Year 2 Suggested Milestones

At the end of each ministry year gather your men's ministry leadership team for a time of evaluations, prayer, preparation, and planning for the next ministry year. For many churches main ministry activity takes place from September through June. Summers are a great time for men to get some rest, renew their spirit, and spend increased time with family.

Develop Your Battle Plan

Using the sample below, begin to schedule out your ministry events and assigned resources. On the following page is a copy from Joshua's Men a local churches one-year battle plan for September 2006 through June 2007.

SUMMIT MEN'S MINISTRY EVENT CALENDAR FOR 2006 / 2007

Date				Event/Title	Point Man
Thursday	Friday	Saturday	Sunday		
			9/10	Kickoff Sunday, J'Men cook breakfast for both services	Chris
	9/15	9/16	9/17	Weekend in the Woods	Chris
9/21	9/22			1 - A Man and His Mirrors	
		9/23		Men's Breakfast (What we need to know about women)	Jay
9/28	9/29			2 - What Men Need to Know About Women	
10/5	10/6			3 - Engaging Your Women Successfully	
10/12	10/13			4 - Staying Close to the Woman You Love	
10/19	10/20			5 - Improving Your Sex Life	
10/26	10/27			6 - How a Man Makes the Money Work at Home	
11/2	11/3			7 - The Good Life and Where to Find It	
11/9	11/10			8 - What Every Dad Needs to Know	
11/16	11/17			9 - Dad's Game Plan for Raising Son's & Daughters	
11/23	11/27			Thanksgiving Holiday	
11/30	12/1			10 - Maximum Parenting	
		12/2		Celebration Dinner	Jay
12/7	12/8			11 - A Man and His Work	
		12/9		Men's Breakfast (What every Dad needs to know)	Bryan
12/14	12/15			12 - Two Visions of Work	
12/21	12/22			Christmas Holiday Season	
12/28	12/29			Christmas Holiday Season	
1/4	1/5			Christmas Holiday Season	
1/11	1/12			13 - Coming Alive at Work	
1/18	1/19			14 - Making a Name for Yourself at Work	
1/25	1/26			15 - Taking God to Work	
2/1	2/2			16 - Launching a Lifelong Winning Streak	
2/8	2/9			Break	
2/15	2/16			1 - Examine the Ultimate Model of Masculinity	
2/22	2/23			2 - Journey into Godly Manhood	
		2/23	2/24	SSeaCMM Men's Retreat - The Great Adventure	Brad
3/1	3/2			3 - Receive Affirmation from Your Father	
3/8	3/9			4 - Keep One Another Accountable	
		3/10		Men's Breakfast (A man and his Work)	Bryan
			3/11	Go for the Guys Sunday	Jay
3/15	3/16			5 - Wage Warfare with Your Enemy	
3/22	3/23			6 - Join a Band of Christian Brothers	
3/29	3/30			7 - Give Yourself to a Godly Cause	
4/5	4/6			8 - Pursue Righteousness	
			4/8	Easter Sunday	
4/12	4/13			9 - Promote Kingdom Living	
4/12	4/13	4/14		NCMM - Kansas City	Brad
4/19	4/20			10 - Confront Ungodly Thinking	
4/26	4/27			11 - Count the Cost	
5/3	5/4	5/5		Trout Bums Round Up - 2007	Dan
5/10	5/11			12 - Love Your Bride, Love the Bride	
			5/13	Mothers Day	
5/17	5/18			13- Seek Male Greatness	
5/24	5/25			14- Instruct the Hard Lessons	
5/31	6/1			15- Seize the Moment	
6/7	6/8			16- Face Problems Head On	
		6/9		Men's Breakfast (Taking God to Work)	Bryan
		6/10		Annual Leadership Summit	Brad
Color code					
	Men's Frat			Resources:	
	Men's Breakfast			Men's Fraternity - Winning at Work and at Home (16 weeks)	Brad / Jay
	Achieving Godly Masculinity			Achieving Godly Masculinity - Bible Study (16 weeks)	Chris / Jay
	Event				

Figure 1 - Sample Ministry Plan of Actions and Milestones

It may be helpful while completing a hard copy to use different colored pens or markers to distinguish between the different activities. When using the soft copy this won't be an issue. Some considerations before you plan out the entire year.

- ¥ Have a copy of the church calendar (or know the critical dates for other events)
- ¥ Have a copy of the school calendar
- ¥ Know when each holiday is scheduled. Some holidays do not happen on the same day or week in the year.
- ¥ If possible, schedule a ministry leaders planning meeting with other leaders in your church to identify any potential schedule conflicts.
- ¥ Keep in mind to stay flexible. Remember "Semper Gumby" (ever flexible)

By completing the one-year calendar your leadership team and the men of your church can see the main thrust of your men's ministry for the entire year.

Conduct Event Debriefs

As a general rule a men's ministry leader should debrief the team after unique and routine events providing feedback to the group as well as to individual team members. Identify areas for improvement during the briefs and catalog them in a notebook. Key personnel should review the notes prior to the next mission and make all necessary changes for improvement. When circumstances have team members all in one location, use face-to-face communications. When this is not possible, use the best acceptable technology.

Keep Cadence with Change

As men's ministry moves into the 21st century it will require men with vision and know how who can make the necessary shifts in methods and means where appropriate. With the rapid changes in technology men's ministry leaders will need to adapt to rapid changes in the way men communicate. Already men with sons in high-school or college are learning to text message as a routine form of communication.

Along with rapid changes in technology creative leaders will need to find creative ways for men to relate with one another. The function of the church has not changed since Christ uttered His famous words in Matthew 28:18-20.

Adopt a Sustainable Discipleship Strategy

Effective men's ministries strategically organize different types of gatherings that work together as a whole. The funnel model illustrates how they fit with each other. There are six distinct types of entry points for men: special events, men's conferences, training seminars, congregational meetings, small group meetings, and man-to-man sessions.

Figure 2 - The Funnel Model

When your men's ministry provides a variety of entry points, you make it easier for men to get involved. The men in your church are in different seasons of life and have different interests. How much they get involved will depend on their interest in spiritual things, their readiness, the time they have available, and whether or not they see value in what is offered.

Another important consideration is the goal for your entry points. Each point should provide an opportunity for men to grow in their relationships with other men. Some events will seem more appealing than others. One big thing you want to avoid is appearing boring and irrelevant. Over and over men's surveys rank these as the biggest reasons why men dislike going to church. Each of the following entry points has implications for your church.

Men's Special Events

Men's special events are strategically designed to be a non-threatening environment for men, especially men outside the church. Most men like non-threatening types of events. This is similar to how they grew in relationships as young men in school. These activity-oriented events offer opportunities for men to become acquainted with each other.

Examples include:
- Outdoor events
- Recreational events
- Sporting events

Implications: Special events are a great place for men to bring un-churched friends, new men in the church, or those not yet involved.

For a significant amount of your men, this will be the first point of contact with other men in the church. Men at these events communicate on the level of "what they do" and begin to interact with others based on what they have in common. Often special events provide an opportunity for a man to move from spectator to participant.

Special events are critical first steps for men who need a non-threatening experience where other men will not ask them to do something for which they are not prepared or at that point willing to make. For example, this is not the kind of event to ask a guy to break into a small group or share a personal struggle. Guys on the fringes of your church or in the community are more likely to attend a special event.

Men's Conferences

Men's conferences are an excellent type of event for the local church. These kinds of events act as a catalyst to motivate men and help light a fire to get things going. Use this kind of event to jump-start your ministry to men.

Examples include:
- Iron Sharpens Iron
- God Men
- Promise Keepers

Implications: Many of the men who attend a male only regional conference return from these events having made a life changing commitment to serve Jesus Christ, their families, friends, and their local church.

When the local church captures the momentum from a men's conference it strengthens the churches mission, families, and leadership. After men return from a regional conference, local men's ministry has a perfect opportunity to capitalize on the spiritual momentum by offering entry points right away into men's small groups, monthly men's breakfast, or other activities.

Men's Training Seminars

Men's ministry workshops, equipping study guides, and training seminars offer men the opportunities to develop in areas specific to being a Christian man. God calls all of His men to grow in their leadership roles. Men who have developed a friendship through a special event or a men's conference are more likely to accept an invitation to attend training or equipping seminars. He will have already experienced some sort of event with men whom he can car pool, laugh, or share something about his personal life. Additionally, focused training is an excellent opportunity for a local church to invest in their men's personal growth, ministry vision, and leadership skills.

Implications: In addition to serving as a good entry point, a seminar provides encouragement, practical tools, and training not always available at a regular worship service.

Examples include:
- Men's Ministry Leadership
- Fathering
- Evangelism and Discipleship

Men's Congregational Events

Men's congregational gatherings provide events where your men can meet for practical teaching from Scripture, fellowship, and prayer. A men's only congregational meeting should have a masculine context that helps men with practical teaching from the Bible specifically as it relates to male issues. This kind of event helps men develop relationships with other men and deepen their relationship with God. Men start to interact more on the level of "who he is" and not just "what he does." Examples include:

- Men's Breakfast
- Men's Retreats
- Go for the Guys Sunday

Implications: This type of gathering gives your men a taste of what can happen in a men's small group. A men's small group is an excellent next step.

Men's Small Groups

Men's small groups usually consist of 3-6 men that are designed to meet on a regular basis for discussion, prayer, and processing the Christian life. This type of entry point offers the local church increased potential for growth. Within small groups men face the challenge of being vulnerable, helping their brothers, and encouraging men with struggles. Communication at this level moves from "what he does" and "who he is" to "what he struggles with" and "what does a man need to succeed." Examples include:

- Inductive Bible Study
- Book reading and study
- Men's ministry videos

Implications: Commitment to a small group helps men resolve problems that arise from being isolated in life. They provide an environment where men can grow in Christ and where men can share ways to minister to their families, friends, church, and community.

Man-to-Man Sessions

Man-to-man sessions give a man the strongest opportunity to grow in his relationship with another man and his relationship to God. This type of ministry is built with a solid commitment to learning how to apply God's Word, and relate deeper with another man. Ultimately, a man who disciples another man one-on-one, raises up a laborer who goes into the harvest fields of men's souls. The connection between man-to-man sessions is total trust as the mentor trains a protégé in the principles of discipleship and equipping for ministry.

Implications: Through one-on-one discipleship men grow into mature disciples. They receive focused training and deeper accountability. Through equipping, men grow to take on more important leadership roles and responsibilities.

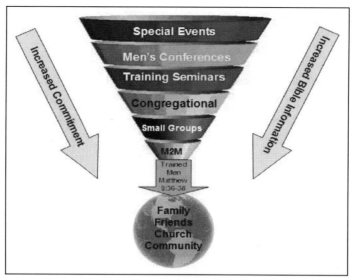

Figure 3 - Progression through the Funnel

Guide Men through the Funnel

As a funnel provides a narrowing parameter for putting liquid into a container, so the funnel demonstrates the progression of a man's involvement in the local church. For successful progression men must understand the need for increased commitment and biblical information. The left side of the funnel represents an increased commitment; the right side of the funnel represents increased biblical information. As the events progress down the funnel, they require a greater degree of commitment and they impart a greater degree of biblical information. The main goal of an effective ministry to and through its men, is to help them transfer biblical truth into every day application as they lead their families, grow in friendships, impact their churches, and change their communities. In the end they become laborers in the harvest fields of the earth (Matthew 9:36-39).

Make Disciples and Disciple Makers

All your events and efforts should have a specific purpose in building the team and ministering to your men. On Figure 3 note the upper half illustrates the strategy for making disciples. This focus is ministry *to* your men. The lower half illustrates the strategy for making disciple makers. This focus is on ministry *through* your men.

A man's relationship with his family reflects his true dependence on God and long-term spiritual influence. Can you imagine a church without healthy marriages (Ephesians 5:25)? Can you imagine healthy marriages without healthy men? Can you imagine healthy men without the fundamentals of the Christian faith? Having an intentional disciple making strategy for the men of your church is the key to a truly healthy church.

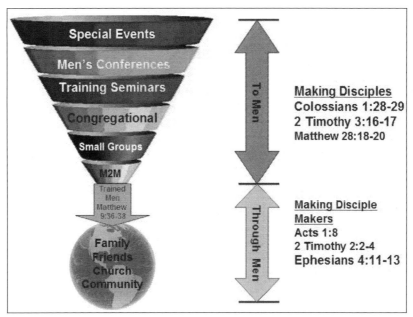

Figure 4 - Ministry to and through Men

The future of your church is dependent on the next generation. Trained, godly children who are spiritually maturing will lead your church someday. ("Train up a child in the way he should go, even when he is old he will not depart from it." Proverbs 22:6) Fathers have a vital role in this process.

All that a man has is given to him by God. Men should be willing, in turn, to give to their church through their attendance, prayers, service, and financial contributions. Intentional leadership development of your men and the exercise of their spiritual gifts are essential to the health of your church (1 Peter 5:2).

The budgets, programs and the leaders of men's ministries who reflect a high commitment to outreach and evangelism, both locally and worldwide, set the pace for your church. Significant numerical growth through evangelism is an expected outcome of this commitment. As the men in your church reach out to friends, neighbors, co-workers, and others in the community, your church's ministry is multiplied (Luke 19:10).

The key principle is to make sure that all of the ongoing activities that you offer for men are helping them become disciples and disciple makers.

Define Your Ministry Purpose

Pat Morley from Man in the Mirror has done an outstanding job of capturing the elements that make men's ministry happen in the local church. The momentum cycle illustrates the cycles that all men's ministry go through.

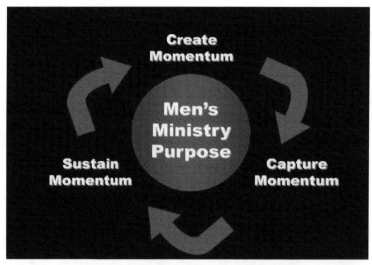

Figure 5 - Men's Ministry Momentum Cycle

A ministry purpose affects everything you and your ministry does. Jesus said, "Therefore go and make disciples of all nations, baptizing them in the name of the Father and the Son, and the Holy Spirit, and teaching them to obey everything I have commanded you. And surely I am with you always, to the very end of the age." (Matthew 28:19-20). The Great Commission is at the heart all the ministries in the local church. So, what is the overriding purpose of your ministry to men? It should be to make disciples who will make disciples.

The purpose of men's ministry is much greater than just helping men be better husbands, fathers, and workers. While each of these are critical needs in a man's life, they are not the biggest need nor the central reason a local church should have an effective and efficient ministry to and through its men.

A men's ministry purpose statement gives your men a clear vision and mission to all your events. The vision is the biblical mandate for ministry. It is the overarching reason you do ministry. The mission statement should bring into view the specifics of what you believe God has called you to accomplish.

The key to getting a stationary man moving is to create value for him. Know your men and their needs, and then reach them in ways that are relevant to their lives. Keep in mind that provision follows vision. Men will give to and actively support a biblical vision and mission.

Create Momentum

When you create value with an activity you create momentum. Like a gear that makes a wheel turn, so doe's momentum to your ministry. Typically the first two layers of the funnel tell men what to do in their Christian lives as they help create momentum. After attending an event where they hear and learn the things to do they are ready to understand the how to do.

Capture Momentum

Capture Momentum by providing the right next step. Don't create momentum without a plan for how you will capture it. Make the follow-up fit the event, right size the commitment you are asking for, have an ending point, help men take the next step. NOTE: if you consistently fail to capture momentum when you create it, you will not build a sustainable ministry. *Always show men a next right step.* The third and fourth layers of the funnel help men understand the how's in the Christian life. These ministries are a great way to help capture momentum.

Sustain Momentum

Sustain momentum through relationships. Men tend to fail when isolated. Together, they can become genuine disciples who can transform the world around them. First, help them uphold their spiritual progress. Second, help them with regular prayer and Bible study. The key is helping them become and stay mature in Christ.[ii] The fifth and sixth layers of the funnel model provide men with whom will help them in their Christian lives. These layers are great ways to help continue momentum.

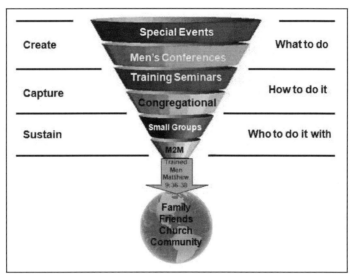

Figure 6 - Momentum Applied to the Funnel

At your starting point the baseline of established disciples forms the foundation of your ministry.

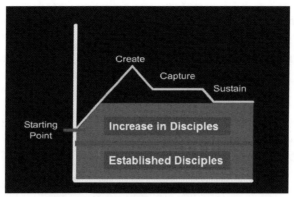

Figure 7 - Men's Ministry Momentum Graph

Through creating, capturing, and sustaining momentum, you will increase your baseline of established disciples. However over time you may see some men drop off. It is normal for life and ministry to happen in cycles. Some men will need several cycles to continue their growth. Not all of them will be involved in small groups or man-to-man types of events.

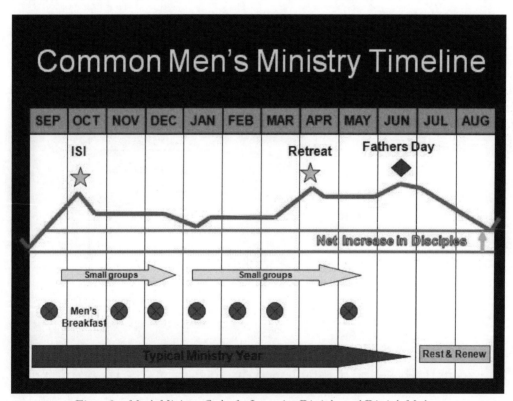

Figure 8 – Men's Ministry Cycles for Increasing Disciples and Disciple Makers

If you continue to apply these principles over time, you will have new men staying involved in your discipleship process as well as disciple makers. This includes a growing and loyal men's ministry leadership team. Each year you will have a net increase in men disciples.

NOTE: Part of the charter of a great men's ministry is to raise up laborers for the other parts of the local church. It is normal for some men to leave the leadership team and move into working with young men in the youth group or teaching boys in Sunday school. If you have done your job these men are moving on to exercise their gifts of making disciples where they see a need.

Mobilizing Men to a Men's Ministry Event

Most of what happens in a ministry to men will take place in and around the local church; however, occasionally there are offsite events that help local churches build into a men's ministry. For example, men's regional conferences are an excellent type of catalyst event. These kinds of events motivate men and help light a fire to get things going. Many of the men who attend a male only regional conference return from these events having made a life changing commitment to serve Jesus Christ, their families, friends, and their local church. So, how does a local church mobilize men to an offsite event? Here are seven practical principles for mobilizing men:

Principle 1: Solicit Prayer - Ask God to mobilize the men of your church to go to the event. Solicit prayer from men, women, boys, and girls.

Principle 2: Designate Champions - Delegate leadership of this event to a couple of champions who have a passion for the event and stature with the other men in the church.

Principle 3: Use a Game Plan – Use a game plan based on some best practices for churches who have successfully mobilized their men to an event (see next page for sample). Using a game plan provides step-by-step timed actions and required resources. It is also easy to modify.

Principle 4: Register as a Group - Make the event your own by registering men as a group. Set up a station outside the sanctuary and stack it with promotional materials. Personally invite men face-to-face, with email, and solicit over the phone. Promote the event using media materials such as a video or power point. Set up call teams so that every man in the church receives a personal invitation. Pass out invitation cards.

Principle 5: Travel Together - Make the event your own by attending the event as a church group. Some guys really enjoy meeting for coffee or breakfast before heading out for the event. Recruit car captains who will invite men and coordinate travel for three or more riders. Get there early enough to meet together at the event. Plan on eating lunch together and use the time to process the conference subjects with each other. Most church locations allow tail-gate parties and cooking.

Principle 6: Follow Up the Event- Make the event your own by planning ahead to follow it up. Some guys like to meet for dinner or coffee on the way home. Consider having one or two men give a personal testimony the following Sunday morning or at the next men's breakfast. Set up an in house men's event within the next month to discuss the content and application. Provide the attendees with a small group next step within thirty days after the event.

Principle 7: Set an Example - Pastors your participation speaks volumes to the men. You need to be there! More men will attend when you lead the way than when you send someone else to lead them for you.

An offsite event can serve as a great resource and catalyst for your ministry to men. These events allow your leadership team to focus on relationship building and inviting men to join them versus expending most of their energy putting on an event. Going forward, consider a regional conference in the fall and a regional retreat in the spring as part of the men's ministry calendar.

Mobilizing Men Game Plan

Provided by Iron Sharpens Iron (**www.ironsharpensiron.net**)

Timeline	Action items to mobilize men to the event and to build momentum for your ministry to men	Resources your team needs
7 weeks	Put up posters (do not overlook the men's restroom) Start soliciting prayer from men and women! Introduce the event to your church. Update your church web site to include event.	• Posters • eMail
6 weeks	Place event brochures at church for men to review. Make short pulpit announcement. Play DVD or display PPT presentation.	• Brochures • Power Points/DVD
5 weeks	Verify posters are located in public places for men to see. Print and insert into church bulletin #1, make short pulpit announcement that sign ups begin next week. During the week send your men an email linking them to your church site, sponsor site or church site. Continue to solicit prayer.	• Insert Bulletin • Brochures • eMail
4 weeks	Announce sign up begins today. Ensure pastors and leaders sign up first. Repeat one min pp presentation or promo DVD. Have men at table outside sanctuary. Call the South Seattle Coalition of Men's Ministries if you need more brochures.	• Sign Up Sheet • Table & Volunteers • Power Point/DVD • Brochures
3 weeks	Continue Sign-ups. Present the 1 min pp presentation or show the video clip. Staff the signup table. Buy a 30 x 48 poster board. Transfer names of the men on the sign up sheet to the poster board. Email men and ask, "Did you sign up?" Include soft copy of event. Continue to solicit prayer.	• Power Point/DVD • Table & Volunteers • Phone • Poster board • Sign up sheet
2 weeks	Continue Sign-ups. Make announcement that next Sunday is last day to sign up. Insert bulletin #2. Staff the signup table. Review who is going and who has yet to decide. Make calls and send eMails to all undecided. Send email "Sign up ends this Sunday."	• Phone & eMail • Brochures • Sign up sheet • Table & Volunteers
1 week	Make announcement this is final Sunday to sign up. Staff table and extend invitations. Insert bulletin #3. Collect any unpaid funds.	• Table & Volunteers • Sign up sheet • Bulletin
Month - Day	**Attend Regional Iron Sharpens Iron**	• **Your men**
Post 1-2 weeks	Provide an opportunity for men to testify to what they are applying as a result of this event. Provide next steps for men to continue in ministry.	• Date • Place
Post 2–3 months	Schedule a dinner or breakfast for all volunteers, staff, and any local seminar presenters to attend. Discuss evaluation content and feedback.	• Date & Place • Evaluations

Table 3 - Mobilizing Men Strategy

Training a Men's Ministry Team

Men in relatively new leadership positions may feel a bit insecure when starting to perform their agreed role in men's ministry. Providing quality training for them develops their skill and knowledge base as well as equips them to do the job properly. Never ask a man to do anything you aren't willing to train him to do, or for that matter, do yourself.

- *One-on-one.* One-on-one training allows for the greatest level of impact and change in a man's life. Through one-on-one a mentor and protégé exchange dialogue, explore situations, and answer personal questions. All of which may not happen in a small group setting. The following four principles of one-on-one give the mentor a clear method for imparting both knowledge and skills in another man to equip him for ministry.

    - Tell him why: Explain why this task is important to the man, to the team and to the Lord.
    - Show him how: Before giving him the task, have the man watch you complete the task as it is properly accomplished.
    - Get him started: Whenever possible, work with and alongside a man before asking him to do a job by himself.
    - Keep him going: After the man takes on the new role and responsibilities, be sure to periodically discuss the assignment and view the results.

- *Small Groups.* Small groups are extremely effective in training more than one man. As men grow in their relationships, they become more like Christ. Leadership is developed as men move from acquaintance, to friend, and brothers. A by-product of helping men develop leadership in a small group setting is giving preliminary experience for the leader. This is very beneficial in the future when they are called to lead a small group of their own.

- *Books.* There are several excellent books on starting, building, and growing a men's ministry (See resource list in Appendix C). Reading a book and meeting to discuss the content is a great way to provide all the leaders a common foundation of service and ministry. In some individual situations, giving a book helps one or two of your men gain insight into specific men's ministry related issues.

- *Magazines, Periodicals, emails.* Besides books, you can use magazines, periodicals, and online emails to disseminate information to the leadership team. Ask your pastor to pass on any good articles to you for review and forwarding to the team.

- *Videos and DVD's.* DVD's and Videos are excellent tools that give men a medium that appeals to a man's visual senses. In addition, the majority of DVD series do not require extensive preparations. Leaders can review the materials, insert the DVD, and join the team to view the contents.

\ *Seminars/Conferences*. Many regional and denominational conferences provide excellent messages, seminars, and workshops that focus on specific issues related to life and ministry.

\ *Delegate don't Abdicate*. Delegation is the assignment of authority and responsibility to another person to carry out specific activities. However the person who delegated the work remains accountable for the outcome of the delegate work. It allows a protégé to make decisions, i.e. it is a shift of decision-making authority from the mentor to the mentoree. The opposite of effective delegation is micromanagement, where a manager provides too much input, direction, and review of 'delegated' work. Your ministry will only develop and grow as you invest in leaders and delegate the ministry roles and responsibilities. Monitor before judging their performance.

\ *Transfer and Release*. Men need authority, freedom, and resources in able to perform as God has gifted them. To build in men start small and build up with increasing responsibility and authority. Give them a small task to accomplish before assigning a large one. Evaluate their performance, make appropriate suggestions, and learn from their effort how they work, operate and relate to others. Teach them to analyze and solve their problems.
- What has to be done?
- When will it be done?
- Who will help?
- What tools or resources will the task require?

\ *Give them your time, talents, and treasures*
- Be willing to expend your resources for them
- Be a servant to them whenever possible
- Be available to assist them as required
- Ask them questions about their ministry: "How it is going? "What do you need?" "Is there anything you would like assistance with?" Help them identify bottlenecks or potential problems before completing a task. Provide necessary feedback.

\ *Stay in Touch*. Establish communication plans with your leaders. You need to be routinely available to meet with your men to discuss how they are doing both in their personal as wells as ministerial lives. As you give away aspects of your ministry, be available to support and encourage their hard work as men labor in the harvest fields. Find out how you can serve them and make them successful.

\ *Celebrate Victories and Change*. At least once a year, take time to review the ministry to identify the successes over your ministry year. Calculate the lives that were touched and men that were changed as a result of the men's ministry. Setup up a celebration dinner or

BBQ. Pass out awards and gifts with a significant emphasis on thanking them for building up God's kingdom.

Q - Which one are of training do your men need most at this time?

Q - Why?

Training Objectives for a Disciple

Making disciples incorporates visioning, harvesting, and building in men after conversion. This isn't an easy task. Fortunately, Christ provided an example for the church by training His men. At the end of His earthly ministry, He commanded them to go make disciples (Matthew 28:18-20). The need was great then; the need is great today.

The following training topics are designed to help provide instruction for men that are new to the Christian faith or lack disciple making skills. Almost all of the imperatives from Christ in the gospels tell the people of God to develop and live with godly character as the foundation for being a mature disciple. Here are thirty-six topics to help men mature as disciples.

#	The Way of a Godly Man
1	Assess Your Identity - 1 John 5:1-13
2	Pray to God - Matthew 6:5-15
3	Ask for Forgiveness - 1 John 1:1-10
4	Achieve Spiritual Victory - 1 Corinthians 10:1-13
5	Maintain Your Identity - John 15:1-17
6	Learn and Apply God's Word - Psalm 19:1-14
7	Fellowship with God's People - Acts 2: 42-47
8	Seek God's Kingdom - Matthew 6:19-34
9	Give Generously - 2 Corinthians 9:6-15
10	Express Your Faith - Acts 26:1-29
11	Count the Cost - Luke 9:23-27, 57-62; 14:25-35
12	Worship the King - Matthew 2:1-12

Concept: Do the Right Things

Table 4 - Objectives for New Christians

As you help men grow in Christ, keep in mind this quote, "It has been said that the essence of character is being, but the evidence of character is doing. Conduct is simply character turned inside out. Consequently, what we do is what we are.

Dr Ron Fraser of Point Man ministries.

#	The Character of a Godly Man
1	Live By The Spirit - Galatians 5:1-26
2	Pursue Holiness - 1 Peter 1:13-2:3
3	Practice Godliness - Ephesians 5:1-21
4	Imitate Christ's Humility - Philippians 2:1-18
5	Acclaim Christ's Supremacy - Colossians 1:15-29
6	Be a Godly Man - 2 Timothy 2:14-3:9
7	Do the Right Thing - Titus 3:1-15
8	Love Like a Man - 1 Corinthians 12:31-13:3
9	Build Godly Relationships - Ephesians 5:21-6:9
10	Use Your Motivational Gifts - Romans 12:1-8
11	Reside in God's Will - Romans 12:9-21
12	Watch your Heart and Tongue - James 3:1-18

Concept: Be the Right Person

Table 5 - Objectives for Character Development

#	The Mission of a Godly Man
1	Recognize the Trinity - Matthew 3:16-17; 28:18-20
2	Know the Enemy - Ezekiel 28:11-19; Isaiah 14:12-15
3	Wage Spiritual Warfare - Ephesians 6:10-20
4	Fish for Men - Matthew 4:12-35
5	Preach a True Gospel - 1 Corinthians 15:1-28
6	Sow God's Word - Mark 4:1-32
7	Seek the Lost - Luke 19:1-10; Galatians 3:26-4:7
8	Serve Others - Mark 10:32-45
9	Help People In Need - Luke 10:25-37
10	Work Wholeheartedly - Genesis 2-3; Colossians 3:23
11	Develop World Vision - Acts 1:1-9
12	Live by Faith - Hebrews 11:1-40

Concept: Work the Right Goals

Table 6 - Objectives for Multiplication

Patrick Morley in his book on pasturing men provides this definition, "A disciple is someone called to live in Christ, equipped to live like Christ, and sent to live for Christ."[iii] There are numerous programs available to help the local church make disciples. The important point to consider is having a reproductive plan that produces men who live godly focused lives. No one size fits all.

Part II – Relationships

Strengthening Team Relationships

Many ministries start with a great idea and then disintegrate for lack of one major factor; they did not cultivate deeper relationships. Relationships are the backbone of men's ministry. Men are prone to develop elaborate programs around spectacular events yet fail to touch others in a way that makes a lasting impact. If a church wants to see men truly change, it needs to ensure they are growing deeper in a love relationship with God and continually developing brotherhood with other men (Matthew 22:37-40).

Every man has relationships within his sphere of influence. All relationships have a start and an end. Some men know each other for years; some know each other for only a minute or two. Most men go through a similar process as they experience life together. There are four levels to this process: acquaintances, friends, brothers, and Jonathans. Between each stage, men tend to experience problems. Problems act as a filter restricting men from the next stage in the relationship development. Each stage is described below. Figure 9 is a simple diagram that illustrates each stage and the primary filters between each level of friendship.

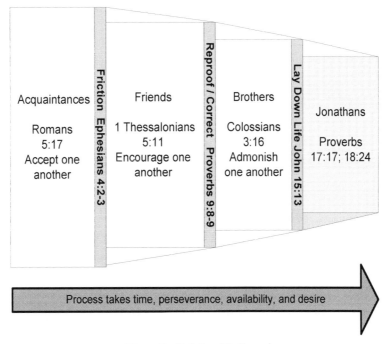

Figure 9 - Relationship Funnel

Acquaintances

Acquaintances are people we meet in our day-to-day lives but with whom we have not developed an intimate friendship. We have occasional interaction with these people. Familiarity is the result of continued acquaintance which develops as people spend increasing amounts of time with one another. For some of us, it is easy to accept people at this stage because we do not know their personal lives. Everything we experience together is on a surface level. A men's ministry team works at meeting men and accepting them for who they are. Romans 15:7 says, "Accept one another, then just as Christ accepted you in order to bring praise to God."

Men tend to develop acquaintances by spending time together on an activity where there is common interest. Communication is on the surface level and often filled with cliché speech. Individuals tend to focus on their own purposes for attending events and keep things about themselves somewhat confidential.

As men grow in their experience and knowledge of one another, they eventually encounter friction in the relationship. Friction can be good and bad. Proverbs 27:17 says, "Iron sharpens iron, so one man sharpens another." Friction tests all relationships. Men either come through this experience as friends, or the relationship stalls.

Friction can take many forms. A few examples are habits, styles, manners, behaviors, pride, and envy. All men experience friction with others. How they work through the friction determines if their relationship progresses to the level of friendship. Intimacy is the result of close connection. Continued intimacy goes beyond the friction and into an established friendship. Keep in mind Ephesians 4:2-3, "Be completely humble and gentle; be patient, bearing with one another in love. Make every effort to keep the unity of the Spirit through the bond of peace."

Friends

Friends are people you know well and regard with affection and trust. Friendships are developed by spending time together, taking an interest in the other person, and encouraging one another. First Thessalonians 5:11 says, "Therefore encourage one another and build each other up, just as in fact you are doing." Communication is at the level of ideas, dreams, and goals. Time together is spent discussing skills, resolving frictions, and addressing conflicts.

True friends will eventually see things that require tough love. Risk is involved at this point. Men either respect their friends for addressing the issue, or they become angry and withdrawn. Proverbs 9:8-9 tells us, "Do not rebuke a mocker or he will hate you; rebuke a wise man and he will love you. Instruct a wise man and he will be still wiser; teach a righteous man and he will add to his learning." Giving reproof, rebuke, and correction in a spirit of love takes discipline and prayer. It is a critical factor in moving the relationship from being a friend to a true brother in Christ.

Brothers

Brothers are men who have the same parents. Men enter into God's family as brothers in Christ. All true children of God are members of God's family. Like members of family, brothers are to support, defend, and help one another. Brotherhood is formed as men develop close relationships. These are the kind of brothers the diagram is referring to. To become part of a band of brothers requires successful passage through the first two stages of building relationships.

A band of brothers is three or more men who share a common vision, mission, and purpose. In the pursuit of achieving their mission, they grow in close interpersonal relationships as brothers. Men allow other men to hold them accountable in the battles of life. Communication flows on a level of strengths and weaknesses. Time is spent together doing things like building a ministry team, worshipping together, and holding one another accountable. Paul describes this type of relationship in his letter to the church at Colosse, "Let the word of Christ dwell in you richly as you teach and admonish one another with all wisdom, and as you sing psalms, hymns, and spiritual songs with gratitude in your hearts to God" (Colossians 3:16). Men who labor together in ministry are more apt to develop into band of brothers. And, a band of brothers who persevere in ministry are more apt to grow into mature disciples. Disciples are men who obey Christ's teachings and are committed to helping others grow in the true knowledge of Christ. This level is one of the most difficult to develop.

Men who are living a life of true discipleship love one another (John 13:34-35). They are men who want to be used by God and strive to see their relationships develop in a godly manner. Men become disciples by learning more about God and His Word and applying Scripture to their everyday lives. Communication is at a level of speaking the truth in love (Ephesians 4:15). Men who are disciples sacrifice for one another as they work together to build up the body of Christ. They know how to function on God's team and demonstrate love to one another like Christ demonstrated love to twelve men on His team.

Jonathans

Proverbs gives us a couple of great verses on deeper male relationships. Proverbs 17:17 "A friend loves at all times, and a brother is born for adversity." Proverbs 18:24 A man of many companions may come to ruin, but there is a friend who sticks closer than a brother. Jonathans are men who are of one heart and soul, as Jonathan and David, and as were the first men on Christ's team. The men on Christ's team lived and labored in close union although they did not start out that way.

To be able to move to the level of being a true Jonathan, every godly man must learn what it means to be broken and die to self. Then He said to them all, "If anyone would come after me, he must deny himself and take up his cross daily and follow me" (Luke 9:23). Just before ascending to heaven to sit at the right hand of the Father Jesus drove home the depth of His relationship with Peter (John 21:15-19). Three times He asks Peter if he loves him. At the end of this discourse Christ says, "Follow Me."

The friends funnel process takes time, perseverance, availability, and desire. With all the demands in life for men, this makes reaching the end process all the more important. It takes a team with heart, vision, and knowledge to produce godly disciples who are willing to lay down their lives for their true friends.

Q – Do you agree or disagree with the Friends Funnel Model?

Q – Why?

Winning Pastoral Support

Men need to know that the senior pastor is 100% behind the ministry to men. This does not mean he has to run the day-to-day operation. Only that he has a visible presence and audible support. Men must honor and respect their pastor by seeking his counsel and release on any men's ministry activities. Your pastor's prayers, presence, and promotions are essential to a successful men's ministry in your church - he "sets the pace" as a leader. Ministries actively supported by the senior pastor grow at a much faster rate and the men live much healthier lives.

- Have you sought your pastor's input and support for your ministry to men?
- If you have senior pastor support, how is he involved in supporting your men's ministry?
- How can the existing men's ministry support and encourage the senior and associate pastor(s) of your church?

Some pastors are afraid to let a man start and build a men's ministry or have an inaccurate understanding of what men's ministry is all about. Here are a few tips to apply when gaining the senior pastors support.

- Set up a meeting with the senior pastor and leaders to discuss men's ministry
- Ask him what he assumes when he hears the phrase, "Men's ministry." Too many pastors associate the term men's ministry with the Promise Keepers movement or worse yet a social club.
- Be sure the pastor and leaders in the church understand that the phrase men's ministry means training men to use their time, talents, and treasures to disciple other men in the local church. It is a process that seeks to build up men who transform others in their homes, communities, and churches.
- After clarifying the term men's ministry, ask the church leadership what their most important goals are for the church. Once the goals are known, explain how men's ministry can help achieve their same goals.
- When the local church executes a men's ministry event, always allow the pastor to have the role he desires to have. Some like being the pastor and speaking a message, others would prefer to take a break and enjoy fellowshipping with the men. Be respectful of his time.
- Demonstrate loyalty to the senior pastor. Be intentional in looking for opportunities to support and serve the pastor. Here are some examples:
  - Prayer support. Set up a team to lay hands on the pastor each Sunday
  - Encouraging emails without criticism. Let him know you are praying for him and the church
  - Mow his lawn or help with some sort of work project around his house
  - Ask him to speak at key men's events like the first or last men's breakfast of the year

Motivating Yourself and the Team

The starting point of motivational leadership is to begin seeing yourself as a role model, as an example to others. One key characteristic of leaders is that they set high standards of accountability for themselves and for their behaviors. They assume that others are watching them and set their own standards according to what they understand based on Biblical mandates.

The world thinks that leaders are those who stride boldly about, exude power and confidence, give orders and make decisions for others to carry out. While a biblical leader must exude confidence and provide direction to his people, he must also demonstrate servanthood. The leader of today is the one who asks questions, listens carefully, plans diligently and then builds consensus among all his team so they achieve their ministry goals. The leader does not try to do it alone. The leader gets things done by helping others to do them. He lives to serve others not to be served. Training men how to be godly soldiers, farmers, and athletes for Christ requires a servant heart.

Good leaders work at motivating themselves and others using common motivation techniques. These are techniques that most leaders can easily learn and apply to further to stand out from the people around them. There are eight key techniques of motivational leaders.

Rewards and Recognition

Rewards for men are often missing from the normal church ministry environment and recognition happens occasionally. These two keys are some of the most powerful motivators at a leader's disposal. *Rewards* do not have to be expensive or extravagant. Reward the team with an occasional dinner or lunch meeting at a classic guy type of eatery. Don't overlook taverns, pubs, or a bar and grill. Purchase small gifts like a book, coffee mug, t shirt, or ball cap. Give them to the guys at key meetings. If you have an annual planning session, this is a great place to give rewards. Some leaders match the reward to the ministry purpose or theme. In this way they get a double blessing. *Recognition* on the other hand can be done throughout the ministry year. Take some time to find a few key moments in the year to recognize each leader's contributions. If the leader is unable to recognize an individual's contributions to the team, something is wrong.

Expectations

Good leaders set realistic expectations up front with the team and team mates. This is by far one of the most underutilized areas in men's ministry. Team leaders need to sit down with each man and clearly define what's expected of them. Setting expectations is not a onetime event or single activity. Tasks, people, environments, priorities, and resources can all change in moment's notice. Good team leaders need to revise and set new expectations throughout the year. Most expectations revolve around three key areas:

1. Key job responsibilities
2. Performance factors and standards

3. Goals

If your team members know what is expected of them, it allows them to focus on results and to monitor themselves against the set standards. Environments in which expectations are not clear, or change from week to week, seldom create high-performing ministry teams.

Vision

This is the one single quality that separates leaders from followers. Leaders have vision. Followers do not. Leaders have the ability to stand back and see the big picture. Followers are caught up in day-to-day activities. Leaders have developed the ability to fix their eyes on the horizon and see greater possibilities. The most motivational vision a leader can have is to be the best he can be as he seeks to serve and obey Christ.

Integrity

This is perhaps the single most respected quality of leaders. Integrity is complete, unflinching honesty with regard to everything that you say and do. Integrity underlies all the other qualities. Your measure of integrity is determined by how honest you are in the critical areas of your life. Integrity means admitting to shortcomings. It means that working to develop strengths and compensate for weaknesses. Integrity means telling the truth and living out the truth; being forthright and direct with difficult people and uncomfortable situations. It means never compromising the truth or biblical standards.

Courage

This is the chief distinguishing characteristic of the true leader. It is almost always visible in the leader's words and actions. It is absolutely indispensable to success and the ability to motivate other people to be the best they can be. For some men it is easy to write out and express a vision for the team; however, the real test of faith is having the courage to follow through on a vision and keep commitments. As soon as a leader sets a high goal or standard, leaders and their teams will run into all kinds of difficulties and setbacks. There is an enemy who is alive and well at hindering the work of ministry to and through men. There will be a lot of temptations to compromise the team's vision, mission, and purpose. There will be an almost irresistible urge to "get along by going along." The desire to earn the respect and cooperation of others can easily lead to the abandonment of principles.

Realism

Realism is a form of intellectual honesty. The realist insists upon seeing the world as it really is, not as he wishes it were. This objectivity, this refusal to engage in self-delusion, is a mark of the true leader. Those who exhibit the quality of realism do not trust luck, hope for miracles, pray for abnormal exceptions to ministry, expect rewards without working, or hope that problems will go away by themselves. These all are examples of self-delusion, of living in a fantasyland.

The motivational leader insists on seeing things exactly as they are and encourages others to look at life the same way. Motivational leaders get the facts, whatever they are. It is critical to deal with people honestly and tell them the truth.

Responsibility

This is perhaps the hardest quality to develop. The acceptance of responsibility means that, as Harry Truman said, "The buck stops here." The game of life is very competitive. Sometimes, great success and great failure are separated by a very small distance. In watching the play-offs in basketball, baseball, and football, the winner is decided by a single point, and that single point can depend on a single action, or inaction, on the part of a single team member at a critical part of the game.

Ministry is very much like competitive sports. Very small things a leader does or does not do can either give him the edge that leads to victory or take away the edge at the critical moment. This principle is especially true with regard to a leader accepting responsibility for himself and for everything that happens to the team. When things go wrong he looks at himself, when things go right he looks at the team.

Excellence

Along with responsibility is demonstrating a spirit of excellence. *A men's ministry that is content with mediocrity is destined for failure.* It is amazing how many people donate old and worn out items to the church but make sure their homes and businesses have new furnishings in great condition. Or, when serving other ministries do a minimum of effort and then leave it to a few people to finish. This attitude fills too many men in too many churches. Whether it is setting up tables and chairs, helping others clean a parking lot, paint a wall, lead a Bible study, make disciples, or serve men a breakfast, it should be done as to the Lord.

The local church should be a place where the highest standards of achievement are aimed for in all of its activity and services. This is especially important where men are concerned. Whenever a ministry produces handouts, study materials, or delivers a service, all the members of the church should see men demonstrating a spirit excellence. Like Army Rangers men should lead the way.

Feedback

Always, always, always start out any feedback session with something positive. Keep in mind the team and or team members are working on goals and standards the a leader has established. Constructive feedback should serve two purposes:

- ᛉ Build on existing strengths of the individual as well as the team
- ᛉ Improve weak or poor performance

Use the following points whenever you need to provide feedback.

- ᛉ *Plan* - This helps develop a framework for providing effective feedback. Think ahead of time about the behavior that should be highlighted and how to help the team member improve.
- ᛉ *Provide examples* - Vague criticism fosters anxiety. Tangible examples are required to highlight the feedback. Do not provide dozens of examples. Make the point with a

couple representative observations. Without a few examples, a leader cannot provide constructive feedback.

\ *Motivate* - The team member may be disappointed by the feedback. Look for opportunities to build the morale of the team member so that he will be eager to improve.

\ *Sandwich* - The team leader should start the session with positive comments, then get to the feedback and finish with positive, motivating comments. Never offer something negative without letting the team or an individual teammate hear something positive. Always open and close any and all feedback discussions by pointing out areas where the team or team member perform well. Reinforce good performance with affirmation and praise. Correct deficient performance with positive feedback and private criticism.

\ *Allow time for feedback* - The process needs to be a dialogue between the team leader and the team member. So, seek feedback from the team member and allow him to agree, disagree or provide his perspective. It is possible that he may have mitigating factors that a team leader was not previously aware of. In the case of addressing an entire team, be careful to mention items that are pertinent to the team. Items pertinent to an individual should be made in private not public. Praise in public, criticize in private.

\ *Set a timeframe for action and follow-up* - The team leader should document any action items, circulate them to the team member and ensure that they are completed. Before the meeting is over, the team or team member should also agree on a follow-up timeframe to check progress.

\ *Plan for follow-up and discipline*. If the feedback does not change a man's behavior, have a second, similar discussion. However, ultimately if there are performance problems that cannot be corrected, the situation will need to be dealt with on a stronger level. Depending on the situation the team member may need to be removed and or replaced by someone else.

Conclusion

The best way for a leader to become a motivational leader is by motivating himself first. Most leaders motivate themselves by striving toward excellence, by committing to becoming everything God desires so they can achieve their maximum potential. A leader motivates himself by jumping into ministry with a whole heart striving to do the job with a spirit of excellence. Leaders motivate themselves and others by continually looking for ways to help themselves and others to improve their lives and achieve their goals. Godly leaders work at taking control of their personal as well as professional lives. A godly leader cannot take men where he has not gone himself.

Almost all men like to know their efforts count especially when so much of their time, talents, and treasures are expended toward a ministry cause. A motivational men's ministry leader will do well when he provides a few well placed rewards and honest appreciation for jobs well done.

Q – Which motivational area do you struggle with the most?

Q – With this information, how can you improve the way you motivate your men's ministry team leader or team?

Evolving Team Concepts

Teamwork is a dynamic concept. All teams have a shelf life and go through a process every time they are formed or another member is added to the roster. The five phases are form, storm, norm, perform, and adjourn.

Form

In the first stages of team building, the *forming* of the team takes place. The team meets and learns about the opportunity and challenges, and then agrees on goals and begins to tackle the tasks. Team members tend to behave quite independently. They may be motivated but are usually relatively uninformed of the issues and objectives of the team. Team members are usually on their best behavior but very focused on themselves. Mature team members begin to model appropriate behavior even at this early phase. Supervisors of the team tend to need to be directive during this phase.

The forming stage of any team is important because in this stage the members of the team get to know one another and make new friends. This is also a good opportunity to see how each member of the team works as an individual and how they respond to pressure.

Storm

Every group will then enter the *storming* stage in which different ideas compete for consideration. The team addresses issues such as what problems they are really supposed to solve, how they will function independently and together and what leadership model they will accept. Team members open up to each other and confront each other's ideas and perspectives.

In some cases *storming* can be resolved quickly. In others, the team never leaves this stage. The maturity of some team members usually determines whether the team will ever move out of this stage. Immature team members begin acting out to demonstrate how much they know and convince others that their ideas are correct. While other team members focus on minutiae to evade real issues.

The *storming* stage is necessary to grow the team. It can be contentious, unpleasant, and even painful to members of the team who are averse to conflict. Acceptance of each team member and their differences needs to be emphasized. Without acceptance and patience the team will fail. This phase can become destructive to the team and will lower motivation if allowed to get out of control. Also, the team's ability to resolve conflicts will determine the depth of team member relationships.

Team leaders during this phase may be more accessible but tend to still need to be directive in their guidance of decision-making and professional behavior.

Norm

At some point, the team should enter the *norming* stage. Team members adjust their behavior to each other as they develop work habits that make teamwork seem more natural and fluid. Team members often work through this stage by agreeing on rules, values, professional behavior, shared methods, working tools, and even taboos. During this phase, team members begin to trust each other. Motivation increases as the team gets more acquainted with the assigned tasks and a division of labor.

Teams in this phase may lose their creativity if the norming behaviors become too strong and begin to stifle healthy dissent. In this phase it is easy for the team to begin to exhibit group think or be led by pressure to perform. The team members are expected to take on more responsibility for making decisions and for their professional behavior.

Perform

The next phase is *performing*. These high-performing teams are able to function as a unit as they find ways to get the job done smoothly and effectively without inappropriate conflict or the need for external supervision. Team members have become interdependent. By this time they are motivated and knowledgeable. The team members are competent, autonomous, and able to handle the decision-making process without supervision. Dissent is expected and allowed as long as it is channeled through means acceptable to the team.

The team makes most of the necessary decisions as it gets the work done. Unfortunately, even the most high-performing teams can and often do revert to earlier stages in certain circumstances. Many long-standing teams go through these cycles multiple times as they react to changing circumstances. For example, a change in leadership or the addition of new members may cause the team to revert to *storming* as the new people challenge the existing norms within the team.

Adjourn

The last and final stage of a team is adjourning. In this stage the team decreases its activities. There is a regression to less productive behaviors and a growing separation between team members. The team is terminated by a decision or is allowed to die.

While the above principles describe the cycles of any team, it does not include the leading or influence of the Holy Spirit. Throughout the Bible God has taken groups of men from suffering situations to wining victories. Only a team leader and his team will know when it is right to adjourn a team.

One example of adjourning a team is the end of a small group study. Ending small groups after they have achieved their primary objective is healthy and helps the local church reproduce new leaders and additional small groups (teams).

Q – What stage are you and your men currently working through?

Q – What is your strategy for moving them to the perform stage?

Working Team Environments

Reproduction was at the very core of the Apostle Paul's ministry and must be at the core of all successful ministries in the local church. To a young leader he writes, "And the things you have heard me say in the presence of many witnesses entrust to reliable men who will also be qualified to teach others." (2 Timothy 2:2). If a men's ministry is to grow, it must harness the power of reproducing disciples and equipping leaders.

The apostle Paul led and worked with multiple teams in his missionary journeys and church plants. To succeed in this work, his men were assigned jobs and roles as they labored in the harvest (Philippians 2:25). In training Timothy, Paul uses metaphors to describe working the ministry (2 Timothy 2:1-7). Whenever a team works together, consider these three key types of working environments: serving as soldiers, competing as athletes, and laboring as farmers.

Serving as Soldiers – Making disciples and reproducing leaders is a battle and the enemy will fight you every step of the way. Paul knowing this, tells young Timothy, "Endure hardship with us like a good soldier of Christ Jesus. No one serving as a soldier gets involved in civilian affairs—he wants to please his commanding officer." (2 Timothy 2:3-4). In the 21st century men are easily distracted by new forms of media, job difficulties, and family stresses. Unfortunately hardship is a normal part of living the Christian life. Men need routine reminders to don their spiritual armor (Ephesians 6:10-18), stand firm in the battle, and endure hardships as good soldiers of the cross.

Men must learn how to keep from the entanglements of life that take their focus off of serving God. Like a soldier after he enlists, God's man attends to the ultimate commander's orders. Soldiers of the King give themselves over to His control even though they live and work in the world. They are to focus on the work God calls them to do and avoid any diversions that draw them away from serving the Commander in Chief.

Competing as Athletes – Almost all men like to compete in some way or another. Even in the first century there were forms of athletic competitions. Paul continues to write, "Similarly, if anyone competes as an athlete, he does not receive the victor's crown unless he competes according to the rules." (2 Timothy 2:5). In order to qualify for competition, the athlete must keep himself in good shape and fit for an event. This included proper food, exercise, and self-restraint. To receive the prize, he must compete by adhering to all the rules. God provides His men with competition rules that call His to be good stewards of their mind, bodies, and soul. Every man needs to understand the need for running the spiritual race in his life and living with good order and self-discipline (1 Corinthians 9:25-27).

It is critical to long term spiritual health for men to learn to master their lusts of the flesh, lusts of the eyes, and the boastful prides of life (1 John 1:15-16). When men work at self-control they master these areas and gain the eternal rewards of a righteous life.

Laboring as Farmers – Paul further illustrates the rewards of ministry by saying, "The hard working farmer should be first to receive a share of the crops." (2 Timothy 2:6). In order to produce a crop, the farmer must plow the soil, plant the seed, put down fertilizer, and pray for rain. Only after working the fields for weeks and months does the farmer realize a return for all the hard work put into his fields. Exercise a farmer's patience. It can take a while for an individual or the team to reap a harvest from all the hard work in men's ministry. Many teams labor from three to five years before their team is up and fully running.

Men must learn to work diligently but wait patiently for the fruit. God's will is often filled with seasons where individuals as well as teams labor long hours before they receive the promises and blessings.

Paul emphasized that hardship, struggle, discipline, and labor precede the enjoyment of God's reward. There are no short cuts in men's ministry. If the team is to succeed it must learn together to grow strong in the grace of the Lord Jesus Christ as it works the ministry, makes disciples, and reproduces leaders. May God bless you with rich rewards as you grow in His strength and grace (2 Timothy 2:1).

Q – Which of these three environments does your team tend to work and labor?

Q – Why is it important to incorporate all three in the way you work your teams?

Creating a Masculine Context in the Local Church

The average church continues to see a drop in attendance. Since 1991, Barna's surveys indicate church attendance, Bible reading, Sunday school attendance, volunteering at church, and donating to a church have all decreased for men but increased for women.iv Church experts such as author Dave Murrow point out the shift may be based on the church customizing services to minister to the majority of attendees which are mostly women and children. At the height of the Christian men's movement work in men's ministry appeared to indicate spiritual revival among men. Unfortunately, men were actually leaving the church in large numbers.

Over the last ten years several basic principles have borne fruit in helping men get involved and stay involved with a local church. Based on the authors observation six basic principles concerning the nature of men should be in place in order to create good masculine church environment:

\ *Space* – Men respond when their need for space is honored. One of the first hurdles for men to overcome is closeness. Women view closeness as a positive attribute in relating to others. Men tend to view this as a threat. While women think distance is abandonment, men tend to view this as safety. At first most men feel uncomfortable discussing deep issues and life's challenges. Some of this has to do with the way men relate.

\ *Facts* – Men often communicate by asking questions and seeking facts. As often as possible incorporate questions and answers in the teaching, preaching, and ministering sessions.

\ *Competition* – In general, men compete, women complement. This can lead to an occasional clash of ideas and opinions. Guys are motivated by reaching goals and rising to challenges; however, they should be challenged with achievable, bite-size goals which are based on taking one step at a time.

\ *Logic* – Men more than women process their circumstances one step at a time in a linear fashion. To help men develop relationships, men need clear goals that are identifiable in progressive steps.

\ *Rules over Relationships* – Men are more preoccupied by principles or rules than they are by relationships. They will enter into and develop relationships where structure and freedom are somewhat balanced. All men have the potential for deeper and meaningful relationships which start as acquaintances move into friendships, grow into brotherhood, and occasionally develop as Jonathan and David or Peter and Christ.

\ *Anger* – Men will often express their feelings in anger and rage. Most seldom recognize the symptoms or the reactions until it displays in unhealthy behavior. Guys need to know how to recognize, react, and process feelings of anger. The church should be a safe place to express anger that is controlled and healthy.

Keep these in six differentiators in mind when scheduling and executing a men's ministry event.

Understanding a Men's Ministry Life Cycle

All teams go through life cycles. It is common for a men's ministry to go through multiple cycles from its birth to its death. This section is designed to provide pastors and men's ministry leaders with a high level overview of the cycles and provide some practical helps at each level. As the ministry moves through the cycles it may or may not recognize how it is changing or what to do if the change is negatively impacting the church or the men. Some changes happen overnight while others are more subtle and happen gradually. If leaders do not monitor the status of their ministry they are likely to miss recognizing the need for change until it is too late or the cost to correct the situation is more than they are willing to pay.

There are seven cycles with distinct behavior characteristics at each cycle. Here is a simple flow diagram that illustrates each cycle. The cycle stages are forming, focusing, growing, peaking, institutionalizing, declining, and surviving.

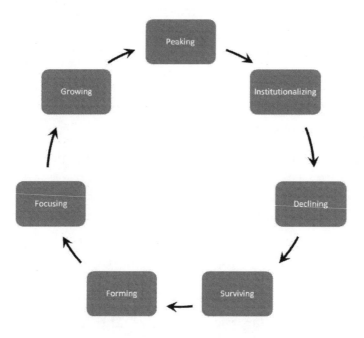

Figure 10 - Ministry Life Cycles

Forming

At this stage one or two men who have an interest in seeing the men of the church form some sort of ministry to and through men start meeting to pray and seek God's will for this ministry. After some prayer and initial planning they look at identifying what will be the primary mission which will drive all the events, activities, and studies.

The founders start to form a core team and identify their men's ministry champion. This may or may not be the senior pastor. Some pastors will make themselves available for men's ministry while others may feel burdened by one more thing they have to take care of. Don't give up on gaining an active support from your pastor. If he has a lot of concerns, start out small and build from there. Be willing to labor for the kingdom.

As the team begins to form the ministry they start out with one or two simple events. Creating an event is a great way to build camaraderie and help form the team's interpersonal relationships. Christ was a master at sending His men on small assignments so they worked together. It is better to start out small with a spirit of excellence than it is to implement too much too fast or with poor quality. Generally speaking ministries that start out small and grow each year last much longer than those who try to jump start a large ministry.

Ministries in the beginning are much easier to mold into shape. The starting lineup wants to find new and exciting ways to get more men involved and active in local church ministry. They are very open to new ideas, methodology, and means for getting the ministry to grow and produce lasting changes in the lives of men.

The guerilla warfare aspect of going into battle over the souls of men and doing something to change lives helps fuel high moral. When two men start a ministry they have a lot of energy and lots of ideas and are trying to get others excited about what they are doing.

Team Suggestions

- Gather the team together quarterly to evaluate the ministry
- Solicit feedback after each event, make it easy to provide feedback and constructive criticism
- Adopt a ministry model that helps the team sustain long term growth
- Seek ways to demonstrate a spirit of excellence in all you do
- Solicit your pastors active involvement
- Clarify your vision, mission, and guiding principles

Focusing

Focusing your men's ministry involves moving from form to a comprehensible focus. The existing men's ministry team has adopted a clear mission statement specifically designed to guide the ministry events, studies, and activities. This is usually a set of biblically based statements that define the ministries mission, vision, and guiding principles.

In this stage the men's ministry champion is leading and inspiring the core leadership team. He works at modeling what he wants for the rest of the church through the men selected for his core team. It is normal for men to still have somewhat of an independent attitude toward doing ministry.

Together the champion and the core team develop a structure for the ministry to build upon. They form a program that helps men enter into more meaningful relationships through organized men's ministry events and activities. Each event and activity is another place where men can come into the church and get more involved.

With a growing structured ministry there is a bigger need for the core team to meet and evaluate all its events, activities, and studies. During this cycle the core team has routine discussions on how they can improve the next time they conduct an event or ongoing study. Improvement is important to the team and they have a desire to see God glorified when they work together to perform a ministry to and through the lives of men.

During a focusing cycle the core team operates under a high moral. Each member of the core team takes on increasing ownership of the services and products.

Team Suggestions

- Adopt a sustainable disciple making men's ministry model
- Ensure your ministry includes working into men and then through men to other people
- Hold annual meetings to evaluate existing ministries and discuss future needs in the church
- Implement new ministries after ensuring you have a qualified man to lead them
- Plan on using multiple mediums to train and disciple the core team
- Administrate a climate survey of all the men who attend the church
- Restrain from attempting to do too much too fast
- Promote your vision and mission whenever possible

Growing

In the growing cycle a men's ministry champion and core team live as disciples and operate as God's men in an effort to fulfill the team's vision and mission. All of the activities and events are in line with the churches overall purpose and everyone senses he is being used by God to bless his church and live a fruitful life.

The men's ministry champion is routinely meeting with his men, consistently sharing the vision and mission statements, and looking for ways to grow the core ministry team. The core team members look for new leaders to help with new ministry opportunities and growing ministry teams.

As the ministry grows the core team looks to expand entry points so they cover multiple levels and with various types of commitments. This is done so they can reach more men in the local church and continue to impact the world. Some activities and events will appear more valuable than others. Each year the core team sees more needs and works to meet them with godly men.

While the ministry is growing there is a consistent need to identify areas for improvements. Each improvement is implemented based on the growing needs of the ministry. Evaluations are a common part of each event and follow-on activities with assigned responsibilities is a normal part of doing ministry work.

The growing moral and enthusiasm is contagious. Most if not all the core team of leaders are setting a visible example to the rest of the men in the church. They are treating one another like Christ treated the men in His ministry. This example inspires other men to start attending events and activities as well as to join the core team.

Team Suggestions

- Continue using the focusing suggestions in this stage as well
- Determine what the majority of men consider of value and be sure to use this in your marketing and publicity
- Ensure all your activities and events have a proper next step
- Reward your men whenever possible by acknowledging their contributions and giving them meaningful gifts
- Evaluate ways to include or involve all the men in the local church
- Adopt a godly form of masculine speech that appeals to men
- Challenge the men to live as intentional followers of Christ
- Provide opportunities for men to give themselves to a cause greater than they are for the rest of their lives

Peaking

Vision and mission focus are at an all-time high with each member of the core team effectively working on ministry tasks. All the events and training programs are well attended. Small groups are routinely meeting and men's lives are being changed. In each ministry men are giving testimonies on what God is doing in and through their lives.

At this stage the men's ministry champion and core team members are interdependent upon one another and work at living like mature disciples of Jesus Christ. Whenever a brother is in need one or more members of the core team offers assistance and help to the point of sacrificing their own wants. Together they relate to one another like Christ related to His disciples.

Systematically the ministry has grown to the point of having sufficient entry points so that any man entering the church could participate at his point of value or level of commitment. Once a man enters into a men's ministry event there is a clear next step in place to help him continue to grow in his understanding of the Bible and his commitment to live as mature disciple of Christ.

The ministries ability to mold itself so it is more effective and efficient has peaked. Routinely new ideas are presented to the team and thoroughly discussed, evaluated, and prioritized. Actions are taken and plans are formed for all that is discussed and decided upon. The champion routinely solicits fresh ideas and new approaches to completing the mission.

The champion and core team members have seen moral reach its highest level. Every man is excited to be on this team of men and to complete his part of this ministry. Each member feels being a part of this team is a calling to something greater than themselves.

Team Suggestions

- Enjoy the time of impact and excitement
- Keep the channels of communication flowing between the leaders and the men
- Stay committed to evaluating and implementing changes that make sense and promote effectiveness and efficiency
- Make sure all the men on the core team know that ministry is about the man across the table
- Keep the one-another's of Scripture in front of them by using multiple mediums: speaking, emails, phone calls, and meetings
- Speak to all your men in masculine terms
- Challenge them often

Institutionalizing

Sooner or later the mission focus starts to slightly diminish. This generally happens when things begin to operate as a routine or recurring process. Forming, focusing, and growing a ministry require a certain amount of structure. Too much structure strangles growth, not enough structure hinders productivity and effectiveness. There is a tension with keeping this balanced and sooner or later things start to slip into a well-established system.

At this stage the core team sees a slight decrease in new men taking on ministries or wanting to be a part of the leadership team. Moral is still fairly high among committed members of the team and ministry is still being accomplished; however, the men begin to sense a lack of fulfillment.

This is the where the ministry starts to lose its focus as a mission to transform men and the people in men's lives to another tradition in which to keep up the momentum. The overall vision and mission purpose for existing is lost in the business of serving and doing the duties of being a man in the local church.

There is a desire to stay structured in what appeared to work in the past. Less change is being proposed by the core team and of the changes discussed there is less being implemented. The members of the core team appear tired and are starting to loose interest in seeing things done with the same enthusiasm as before.

Along with the loss of momentum and purpose, there is a growing polarization of events and programs. Some of the men may be involved in other types of ministries and splitting their time which adds to this issue. Members of the core team may have competing events or programs that become more important than demonstrating unity of the Spirit and cooperation.

Team Suggestions

- Spend some time on surveying all the men who attend the local church
- Pray over the results and factor them into your future ministry to and through men
- Evaluate how you can improve the areas where things are decreasing in effectiveness and efficiency
- Examine any areas where you do not feel the need to be flexible
- Evaluate how each member of the core team is handing their assigned responsibilities
- Consider realigning where appropriate and assigning a new leader if necessary

Declining

At this stage the mission of the core team focuses on maintaining what they already have in place. The team is in maintenance mode not mission mode and all their efforts are to keep things going. Attendance is low and getting men to events is difficult at best.

The champion is frustrated and the core team members are leaving for other ministries or isolating team members by seeking selective support for their ministry activities. Loyal members of the core team still remain.

Ministry activities and events are reduced due to a decrease in interest and attendance. It takes an increasing amount of coordinated contact work to get men to attend existing men's ministry activities.

The core team does little to evaluate the existing men's ministry and expresses strong resistance to any recommended changes. Members routinely express a desire to go back to the methods and activities that worked in the early days. Little time is given to seek constructive feedback or exploration of new ideas.

Those few remaining core team members feel uncertain about how much their contribution is actually making a difference in the lives of others. Polarization of ministries and activities continues to grow.

Team Suggestions

- Spend some time on surveying all the men who attend the local church
- Pray over the results and factor them into your future ministry to and through men
- Realign the leadership team
- If you are the pastor and men's ministry champion, be sure you are not letting burn out effect the ministry and team administration
- Look for areas where men are being tasked versus serving as disciples

Surviving

The objective of what was an organized ministry now looks for ways to keep from dying. Attendance is almost non-existent and no discipleship of men is taking place.

The core team and team leader spend almost all of their energy and time looking for ways to keep things going. Organized events are attended by a few remaining loyalists. Growth has not existed from some time.

Members of the core team do not ask for feedback and seldom meet to discuss ways for improving the ministry. They are close minded toward untested methods, constructive feedback, or new ideas. The team does very little evaluation. Morale is low among the men and if it exists' it exists in a few loyal long term leaders.

Team Suggestions

- Consider letting the ministry die altogether
- Pray and plan over what God has called you to do. If you believe in making men into committed disciples than consider getting a new model with a sustainable strategy
- Gather new leaders who have a fresh perspective on making disciples
- Adopt a new model that has a proven track record
- Give yourself some time to develop the new ministry
- Include a vision that is compelling and offers men an opportunity to be involved with something much greater than themselves

Men's Ministry Life Cycle Summary Chart

	Forming	Focusing	Growing	Peaking	Institutionali-ing	Declining	Surviving
Mission	One or two men seek to identify the primary mission	Leaders have a clear Mission statement to guide the ministry	The champion and core team live and operate to fulfill the teams mission	All members of the core team are effectively working on ministry tasks	Mission focus starts to diminish, ministry starts appearing more routine	More focus on maintaining ministry than fulfilling the mission	Main goal is to keep the ministry from dying
Men	Church forms the core team and identifies a champion	A ministry champion leads and inspires the core team. Men still independent	The core team looks for new leaders to help with new opportunities	Team members are interdependent and live like mature disciples	Shows a slight decline in of newer leaders	Loyal members of the core team remain, most men have found other ministries	Team leader or champion works hard to keep the ministry going
Make up	Starts out with one or two events	Shapes a program with several key entry points	Entry points are expanding to cover multiple levels	There are entry points so any man entering the church could participate	The purpose loses focus as men change from mission to tradition	There is a visible reduction due to decreasing interest and attendance	Any remaining events and small groups are attended by loyalists
Mold	Looking for new ideas	Team routinely meets to discuss existing ministry and ways to improve	Improvements are implemented based on growing needs of the ministry	New ideas are discussed, evaluated, and prioritized	Less changes are proposed, there is a decrease in changes being implemented	Resistance to change is strong with a desire to go back to what worked early on	Closed toward any untested methods or means
Moral	High moral for one or two men who jump start the ministry	Core team operates under high moral and start owning the ministry	The core team is setting a visible example that inspires other men to join	Moral is at its peak, men are excited to be a part of this ministry	There is a growing polarization of events and or programs	Remaining team members feel uncertain and polarization continues to grow	Morale is low except by a few loyal leaders

Table 7 - Ministry Life Cycle Chart

Part III – Operations

Praying Individually and Corporately

Introduction

We maintain personal contact with God through the Word and Prayer. The **Word** is our spiritual food as well as our sword for spiritual battle. It is the foundation for effective Christian living. Through **Prayer** we have direct communication with our heavenly Father and receive provision for our needs. As we pray we show our dependence upon and trust in Him (Navigators Wheel Illustration).

Prayer is ordained for specific purposes. The most important of these is fellowship with God (Ps 84; 1 Jn 1:3). God's answers to prayer reflects the giving nature of His love. He takes the initiative. Fellowship is created as humans respond in adoration and thanksgiving (The Disciples Study Bible pg 1697).

Prayer is God's means of executing His will among humans (Ex 8:30,31; 1 Jn 5:14, 15). Prayer should advance the work of God's kingdom and the growth of God's people (Rom 1:9,10). Prayer is a work of God in which humans participate (The Disciples Study Bible pg 1697).

For over twenty years I have read books, completed bible studies, and participated in various church related prayer activities. This experience led me to create tools, templates and handouts to help keep my prayer life more focused and effective. For some men this type of handout is really helpful. For others, it is binding and a bit too structured. My goal is to help stimulate men to pray. If that end is met, then my efforts are not in vain (1 Cor. 15:58).

Here is a copy of the Christian Soldiers Creed. …. (need to amplify when have time)

Use this guide as a tool for Individual prayer as well as in group prayers…

Christian Soldiers Creed

Recognizing that I was chosen by God to be a soldier and accepting the hazards of spiritual warfare, I will always endeavor to uphold the prestige, honor, and glorious tradition of being a Christian warrior (2 Timothy 2:3).

Acknowledging that a Christian soldier is commissioned to be a militant, a fighter, an aggressive warrior in the attack on the "gates of hell," I must also accept the fact that as a Christian soldier, my Commander in Chief expects me to engage the enemy on my knees, with the shout of victory, *The battle belongs to the Lord!"*

Never shall I fail my brothers! I will always keep myself mentally alert, morally straight, and spiritually strong. I will shoulder more than my share of responsibility in every battle, whatever that may be.

Gallantly I will show the world that I'm a specially selected and well-trained soldier. My Christian demeanor, my readiness for battle, and the care of my equipment, the full armor of God, shall be an example for others to follow.

Energetically I will meet Your enemies upon my knees, Lord. My assigned post shall be the prayer closet. I shall defeat them on the field of battle, for I am continually training and will fight with all my might, remembering "Greater is He that is in me than he that is in the world." *Surrender* is not a Christian word! I will never leave a wounded brother to fall into the hands of the enemy, and under no circumstances will I ever embarrass my fellow warriors in Christ or my Commander in Chief

Readily will I display the intestinal fortitude required to fight on to the Christian objective and complete my mission, even if I be the lone survivor, knowing that my Commander will "never leave me nor forsake me."

Untiringly will I defend the cause of my Commander, on my knees, at my post, knowing that "the prayer of a righteous man is powerful and effective." (James 5:16,17)

Author unknown

Pray for Non-Christians and Public Figures

Most Wanted to Repent and Receive Christ

I recognize prayer for souls is an integral part of any successful witnessing outreach. Only through the Holy Spirit of God are men drawn to the Father through Christ the Savior so I pledge to pray for each individual on this list daily by name. I will do whatever God brings to my attention in helping them to become a true believer in Jesus Christ.

Signature _____

1.	
2.	
3.	
4.	
5.	
6.	
7.	
8.	
9.	
10.	
11.	
12.	
13.	
14.	
15.	
16.	
17.	
18.	
19.	
20	

Pray for Your Public Leaders

1 Timothy 2:1-3 (one a day for an entire month)

1. President of US:
2. Vice President of US:
3. Secretary of State:
4. Secretary of Defense:
5. Secretary of Treasury:
6. Attorney General:
7. Secretary of the Interior:
8. Secretary of Agriculture:
9. Secretary of Commerce:
10. Secretary of Labor:
11. Secretary of Transportation:
12. Secretary of Energy:
13. Secretary of Education:
14. Secretary of Veterans Affairs:
15. Secretary of Health & Human Services:
16. Secretary of Housing & Urban Development:
17. Surgeon General:
18. Speaker of House of Representatives:
19. Majority Leaders of Senate and House
20. Minority Leaders of Senate and the House
21. Cabinet Members
22. Leaders of the White House staff
23. US Senators
24. US Representatives
25. Chaplains of the Senate and House
26. US Supreme Court
27. All branches of the armed forces.
28. State Governor
29. State senators and representatives
30 Elected and top appointed community leaders
31. Schools, teachers, and administrators

Conversational Group Prayer

The Bible urges us to pray, both privately and together. To get the most out of our limited time we suggest a few principles and guidelines for conversational small group prayer. Using conversational prayer in groups leads to an increased consciousness of God's presence and consequently a greater group vitality and unity. It also helps new Christians to fashion their own prayers. The following guidelines are designed to help men get the most out of your small group time for prayer.

Maintain These Guidelines

- Stick to the subject. Pray back and forth on a SINGLE subject, one person or situation at a time, in agreement (Matthew 18-19-20) until the subject is completed.
- Everybody participates who so desires, but no one is forced to participate.
- No one monopolizes. Keep prayers brief, just a sentence or short paragraph. Pray as often as you like, but give AT LEAST one other person a turn before praying again.
- Limit each prayer to one minute maximum. Conversational prayers are concise statements which are stated in *to the point* terms. The 'content' is more important than the 'extent.'
- Periods of silence are OK. Use them to listen for God's voice and sense the Spirit's direction.
- Be brief when sharing your requests. If you take too long sharing your requests, others may not have an opportunity to participate. Get in the habit of keeping your requests short and simple.
- Be aware of God's presence and respond with His purpose:
  - Aware of God who is present with us.
    - Adoration: who **He IS.**
    - Thanksgiving: what **He DOES**
    - Attention: what **He SAYS.**
  - Aware of Our Sin in God's presence. Confession: what I have DONE or FAILED TO DO.
  - Aware of Others from God's point of view. Intercession: what THEY need.
  - Aware of Our Needs Petition: what I NEED.

Enhance Your Participation

An experienced facilitator can enhance conversational group prayer by exercising a few basic principles. Here are some guidelines and principles for the small group facilitator:

- Collect prayer requests as appropriate. Ask the men to provide readers digest versions.
- Encourage all participants to pray.
- Ask someone else to open, be ready to close on time

- Periodically review the guidelines (see Conversational Prayer Guidelines handout)
- Lovingly restrain those who over participate
- Allow for periods of silence
- Enforce the time constraint of one minute maximum for delivering prayers or sharing prayer requests.
- Start and stop your prayer sessions on time
- Implement these guidelines while exercising care and grace to your men

It is inevitable that some members of the group will be more at ease in conversational prayer than others. But nothing will kill a time of prayer more than if one or two members monopolize the prayers either by praying too often or at too great a length. Conversational prayer should give every man equal opportunity to pray and participate. The last page of this document is a handout for you to copy and provide for each man in your small group. May the Lord greatly bless your time and ministry to men.

Use These Examples and Follow This Pattern

Adoration
- "Praise and glory be to you my God. You are exalted above all the Nations."
- "Blessed be your name. A name above all names. That at the name of Jesus, every knee will bow and every tongue confess 'Jesus is Lord'. Oh my God today I worship you."

Confession
- "Oh Lord, please forgive us for not loving others as your word tells us too."
- "Oh Lord, I confess my lust of the flesh, lust of the eyes, and boastful pride of life. Please cast my sin as far as the east is from the west. Renew in me a steadfast spirit."

Thanksgiving
- "I thank you God, for the many blessings you have bestowed on my life and the life of our men here at _____. Thanks for making us men and teaching us authentic manhood."
- "Thanks be to You Oh Lord for _____. We acknowledge our need to give you thanks for everything in our lives is based on your will for us in Christ."

Intercession
- "God, please touch _____ so they can sense your love."
- "Give _____ a desire to love his wife as Christ loved the church."

Petition
- "Lord, teach me to follow Jesus and fish for men."
- "Oh Lord, give me wisdom in dealing with my wife and children. I am in desperate need for your perspective on loving my family with biblical principles."

Scripture Based Prayers

Prayer provides every Christian with direct communication to God. While there are numerous ways and styles for prayer, this document advocates using five key areas. They are Adoration, Confessions, Thanksgiving and Supplication. Supplication can be broken down into two sub areas of Intercession and Petition. Many Christians know this as the popular acronym ACTS. It is easy to remember and provides every Christian with tools to pray in almost any circumstance.

Adoration is praising God for who He is. He created us and desires for us to worship Him. One of the most excellent ways to worship Him is through the use of Scriptures. There are many great Scriptures which describe the attributes of God. Here is one of my favorites "[1] Praise be to the LORD my Rock, who trains my hands for war, my fingers for battle. [2] He is my loving God and my fortress, my stronghold and my deliverer, my shield, in whom I take refuge, who subdues peoples under me (Psalm 144:1,2).

Confession is agreeing with God regarding your lack of obeying God's word. One consistent trait you see when people get close to God is a new revelation of His holiness and their sin. Confession removes the sin and brings us into a right relationship with God so He can speak to us from His word through the influence of His Spirit. "If we confess our sins, He is faithful and just to forgive us our sins, and to cleanse us from all unrighteousness (1 John 1:9). The more time you spend with Him, the more you will discover concerning your need for His forgiveness.

Thanksgiving is thanking God for the good and bad situations in your life. In times of blessing and times of difficulty we are to give God thanksgiving. This means thanking Him even when you don't feel like it. This does not mean you have to be cheerful in your expression. God does not want you to be dishonest. Thanksgiving for your difficult circumstances shows your appreciation and gratitude for what God has done for you in the past and demonstrates your faith in Him for what He is going to do in the future. "In everything give thanks for this is God's will for you in Christ Jesus" (1 Thess 5:18).

Supplication is broken down into two parts: Intercession for others and petitions for yourself. Intercession is praying on behalf of another for their needs. Samuel the prophet loved the people of Israel and provide a great model for all Christians. "As for me, fare be it from me that I should sin against the Lord by failing to pray for you. And I will teach the way that is good and right." (1 Samuel 12:23). Petition is lifting up your own needs before the Lord. As you pray you show your dependence upon and trust in Him. "Casting all you cares upon Him because he cares about you." (1 Peter 5:7).

Spending time in God's word and prayer is the central ways for deepening your understanding of who God is and what He does. The more time you spend with Him the better you will grow in your relationship. The rest of this handout contains sample prayers for you to use as a pattern for your own personal time in the battle for living a godly life. May the Lord richly bless you as you seek to know Him and experience His presence.

Pray Using ACTS

Adoration
- "Praise and glory be to you my God. You are exalted above all the Nations. Be exalted in our daily lives."
- "Blessed be your name. A name above all names. That at the name of Jesus, every knee will bow and every tongue confess 'Jesus is Lord'. Oh my God today I worship you."
- I have seen you in the sanctuary and beheld your power and your glory. Because your love is better than life, my lips will glorify you. Enable me to speak of You throughout the day with words that glorify You."

Confession
- "Oh Lord, please forgive us for not loving others as your word tells us too."
- "Oh Lord, I confess my lust of the flesh, lust of the eyes, and boastful pride of life. Please cast my sin as far as the east is from the west. Renew in me a steadfast spirit."
- Heavenly Father, please forgive me for _____. I confess this as sin and boldly come before Your throne for mercy and forgiveness.

Thanksgiving
- "I thank you God, for the many blessings you have bestowed on my life and the life of our men and women here at _____. Thanks for making us men and teaching us authentic manhood. Thanks for providing a woman to be a suitable help for a man."
- "Thanks be to You Oh Lord for _____. We acknowledge our need to give you thanks for everything in our lives is based on your will for us in Christ."
- "I know all things work together for the good of those who love You and are called according to Your purposes. I thank You for _____."

Intercession
- "God, please touch _____ so they can sense your love and care."
- "Please heal _____ of the emotional scars they have received in life."
- "Today I lift up to You _____. Draw them to You and bring them to a saving knowledge in Christ. Use me to help them see who You are.

Petition
- "Lord, teach me to follow Jesus and fish for men."
- "Oh Lord, give me wisdom in dealing with my spouse and children. I am in desperate need for your perspective on loving my family with biblical principles."
- "Open my eyes so I may behold wonderful things from Your word and be filled with Your inward abiding presence."

Pray The Lord's Prayer

1. Our Father In Heaven

   Heavenly Father, I now come boldly before your throne of grace so that I may obtain mercy and find grace to help in my time of need (Hebrews 4:16).

   By virtue of the blood of Jesus Christ, which was shed on Calvary's Cross, I can call you my Father (John 1:12). Your Holy Spirit bears witness with my spirit that I am your child. You really have replaced my spirit of fear with the Spirit of adoption, whereby I cry "Abba", which means "My Father" (Romans 8:15,16).

2. Hallowed Be Your Name

   Lord God, let your name be set apart from every other name. Some of your names are:

   Jehovah-Rophe (God is my healer) Glorify your name by healing

   _____.

   Jehovah-Shalon (God is my peace) Glorify your name by quieting the storm of anxiety in my heart and give me peace.

   Jehovah-Jireh (God is my provider)

   Glorify your name for so graciously providing for me in the past and I thank you in advance because you will continue to do so in the future.

   Jehovah-Nissi (God is my banner of victory)

   Glorify your name for being my shield of security and strength. Your banner over me is love

   Jehovah-M'Kaddesh (God is my sanctifier)

   Glorify your name by setting me free from my sins

3. Your Kingdom Come, Your Will Be Done

   Father, I pray that I would know your will for my life today (Romans 12:1,2)

   I pray that you would give me the desires that you want me to have (Psalm 37:4)

I pray for my family, our Church and our nation (1 Timothy 2:1,2)

I pray for the spreading of your Kingdom as you open doors for our message, so that we may proclaim the mystery of Jesus Christ, and that we may proclaim this message clearly (Colossians 4:3,4)

4. Give Us Today Our Daily Bread

Oh Lord, help me focus on today's needs, not tomorrow's (Matthew 6:34)

Provide my daily need for more of You.

Help me wrestle through my problems with _____. Like Jacob your servant, I will not let go until You have blessed my life (Genesis 32:25,26).

Father I pray that the Holy Spirit would fill my life with power and purpose today (Acts 4:31).

Father, guide me to pray for needful necessities and not needless luxuries (James 1:5; James 4:2).

5. Forgive Us Our Sins As We Forgive Others

Your word says that the Blood of Jesus cleanses us form all sin (1 John 1:7). Father, I confess my sins of _____, you are faithful and just to forgive my sins, and to cleanse me from all my unrighteousness (1 John 1:9).

Father, help me to forgive and release others (Matthew 6:12-15).

Father, I pray for _____ who has mistreated me. Set my will to forgive that person.

6. And Lead Us Not Into Temptation, But Deliver Us From the Evil One

Father protect me and my family this morning. Help us to resist the devil and force him to flee from us by drawing closer to You (James 4:7).

Father, should any temptation grip me this day, you are faithful and will not allow me to be tempted beyond what I can stand. You have promised that with each temptation you will provide a "way of escape" (1 Corinthians 10:13). Please show me your way out, Lord.

7. For Yours Is the Kingdom, and The Power and Glory Forever

O Lord, Yours is the greatness and the power and the glory and the majesty and the splendor, for everything in heaven and earth is yours. Yours O Lord, is the kingdom; You are exalted as head over all. Now, my God I give you thanks and praise your glorious name (1 Chronicles 29:11,12).

That at the name of Jesus every knee should bow, in heaven and on earth and under the earth, and every tongue confess that Jesus Christ is Lord, to the glory of God the Father (Philippians . 2:10,11).

Pray on full Armor of God

Read Ephesians 6:14-18 as a model for praying on the full armor of God.

"**Stand firm then** "Oh great and mighty God, help me keep my feet firmly planted in the face of your enemies as I go throughout the day serving as Your soldier."

- **with the belt of truth buckled around your waist**, "Around my waist I wrap the belt of your truth which supports the small of my back, keeps me balanced and protects vital organs."

  -**with the breastplate of righteousness in place**, "Over my chest I place the breastplate of righteousness. Not my righteousness, but the righteousness of Christ. Protect me from the blows of the enemy."

- **and with your feet fitted with the readiness that comes from the gospel of peace**. "On my feet I place sandals of readiness. Show me where You are at work and enable me to share the gospel of who You are and what You have done to save men from their sins."

- **In addition to this, take up the shield of faith, with which you can extinguish all the flaming arrows of the evil one**. "In my one hand I place the shield of faith to use against the onslaught of flaming arrows sent by Your enemies. Show me when and where to raise this shield. Enable me to see the enemies attack and so properly defend myself by having faith and trust in only You."

- **Take the helmet of salvation** "I place the helmet of salvation over my head. Protect my mind from being impacted by the world, the flesh and the devil. Keep my mind focused on serving You and the mission You have provided for me to live in a day to day service."

- **and the sword of the Spirit, which is the word of God**. "In my other hand I place Your sword of the Spirit which are words You have spoken. Enable me to properly wield the sword as a good soldier of Christ Jesus. Show me how to apply the words You speak and become more like Your Son.

- **And pray in the Spirit on all occasions with all kinds of requests**. "Fill me with your inward abiding Holy Spirit so I may lift up prayers as I go throughout the day serving You. Enable me to pray without ceasing, always giving thanks for the days events since they are Your will for my life."

With this in mind, be alert and always keep on praying for all the saints." "Open my eyes to see You and continually sense Your presence and purpose throughout the day. Help me be a man alert to opportunities, ready for action and committed to fulfill my duties. This morning I pray for all the men and women in our body and ask you give me reminders throughout the day for specific prayers on their behalf. Blessed be the Lord my Rock, Who trains my hands for war, and my fingers for battle (Psalm 144:1).

Pray for Your Pastor(s)

Christian leaders are always in need of God's protection and presence. Here are 31 prayers for pastors and Church leaders. There is one for each day of the month.

1. That Your eyes are on my Shepherd(s). Your ears are attentive to prayers and Your face is against all those who plot evil against _____ (1 Peter 3:12).

2. _____ would have discernment in seeing any schemes of the enemy against our body (Ephesians 6:11,12).

3. For _____ to be still before You and to wait on You (Psalm 27:14).

4. Set Your angels about _____ and allow no power of the enemy to harm _____ (Ps 91:11).

5. For _____ to have a discerning mind to prioritize the precious minutes of the day. Guard _____ against being distracted from his calling (Psalm 90:12).

6. _____ would glory in the cross (Galatians 6:14).

7. Keep _____ holy in every way. As my pastor(s) draw near to You, draw near the my pastor(s) (Heb 10:22).

8. That the eyes of _____ may be enlightened to know the hope to which we are called and the riches of our glorious inheritance as saints. Let my pastor(s) know the incomparably great power which is us who believe (Ephesians 1:18,19).

9. That you would lift up the hands of _____. Place them in the shelter of the Most High to rest in the shadow of the Almighty. Be my pastor(s) refuge and fortress (Ps 91:1,2).

10. That stress, demands and fatigue would not hinder _____ from serving You. Give my pastor(s) vision, godly dreams and hope for fulfilling Your will (Philippians 4:19).

11. _____ would forgive those that hurt them and speak against them. Enable my pastor to confront church controllers, yet still love them with Christ's love (Ephesians 3:32-5:1).

12. Guard _____ from futile thinking and vain imagination (Ephesians 4:17). Enable my pastor(s) to take every thought captive to the obedience of Christ (2 Corinthians 10:3-5).

13. You would enable _____ to be an oak of righteousness, a planting from You to display Your splendor to our people (Isaiah 621:3)

14. _____ would be kept in the middle of good and exciting worship. Keep _____ from the traditions of men and religion that hold a form of godliness but deny its power (2 Timothy 3:5).

15. You would give _____ a vision of heaven (Isaiah 6).

16. _____ would be men after Your own heart, who would accomplish all Your will (Acts 13:22).

17. Cause the mind of Christ to be strong in _____ thinking (1 Corinthians 2:16).

18. Cause _____ to rise everyday to seek You (Mark 1:35) and be devoted in prayer (Col. 4:2; Rom 12:12).

19. Bless _____ with a rich study time in Your word. Illuminate the Scriptures to fill _____ with your inward abiding Spirit (2 Timothy 2:15; Psalm 119:18).
20. _____ would preach sermons that are pleasing in Your sight (Psalm 19:14).

21. _____ would fear only You and live in complete obedience (Proverbs 19:23, John 14:21).

22. _____ would be men filled with Your Holy Spirit. That all of my pastor(s) actions would demonstrate faith and love (Ephesians 3:14-19).

23. Protection for _____ and their family. Bind Satan and his host of heavenly powers from touching _____ or their families (1 Peter 5:8,9).

24. _____ would be men who know You and are sensitive to Your leading (Philippians 3:10).

25. Give _____ good health (John 16:24).

26. _____ family relationships would be loving, unselfish, respectful, honoring, guiding and harmonious (Proverbs 20:7).

27. _____ would be devoted to prayer and ministry of Your word (Acts 6:4).

28. _____ would bear spiritual fruit that would last for eternity (Galatians 5:22,23; John 16:16).

29. _____ would promote and participate in ministries to equip the saints for service and discipleship (Ephesians 4:11-13).

30. Impact and convict our congregation to regularly pray for _____ and their families (1 Thess. 5:25).

31. That our congregation would not impose on _____ unrealistic expectations (1 Thess. 5:13).

Pray to God the Father, Son, and Holy Spirit

Jehovah Jireh – The Lord Provides. God, in this Your love was manifested to us, that You sent Your only begotten Son into the world, that we may live through Him. Gracious are You Lord, and righteous; yes, You are merciful. You have delivered my soul from death, my eyes from tears, and my feet from falling. O Lord, truly I am Your servant. I will offer to You the sacrifice of thanksgiving, and will call upon Your name (1 Jn 4:9; Ps 116:5,8,16,17).

Jehovah Rophe – The Lord Heals. Surely You have borne our griefs and carried our sorrows. You were wounded for our transgressions, bruised for our iniquities; the chastisement of our peace was upon You and with Your stripes we are healed. In Your own self You bore our sins in Your body on the tree, that we being dead to sin should live to righteousness. There is salvation in no one else; for there is no other name under heaven that has been given among men whereby we must be saved (Is 53:4,5; 1 Ptr 2:24; Acts 4:12).

Jehovah Nissi – The Lord Our Banner. Yours, O Lord, is the greatness and the power and the glory and the victory and the majesty, indeed everything that is in the heavens and the earth. Yours is the dominion, O Lord, and You do exalt Yourself as head over all. In Your hand is power and might; and it lies in Your hand to make great and to strengthen everyone. Now therefore, my God, I thank You and praise Your glorious name (1 Chron 29:11-13).

Jehovah Rohi – The Lord My Shepherd. You guide us in the paths of righteousness for Your name's sake. We will fear no evil; You are with us. You prepare a table before us in the presence of our enemies. You anoint our heads with oil; our cup runs over. You have sent the Helper, the Holy Spirit, in Your name, and He teaches us all things, and brings to our remembrance all You have said. He guides us into all truth (Ps 23:3-5; Jn 14:26; 16:13).

Jehovah Shalom – The Lord Our Peace. Your Name is Wonderful Counselor, the Mighty God, the Everlasting Father, the Prince of Peace. If You are for us, who can be against us. You who spared not Your own Son, but delivered Him up for us all, how shall You not with Him freely give us all things? You have justified; who shall lay anything to our charge? Who shall separate us from Your love, which is in Christ Jesus our Lord? Lord, you have given strength to Your people; Lord You have blessed Your people with peace (Rm 8:31-15; Is 9:6; Ps 29).

Jehovah Tsidkenu – The Lord Our Righteousness. Righteous are You, O Lord. Your righteousness is an everlasting righteousness, and Your law is truth. Your right hand is full of righteousness. Lord God, You are righteous in all the works You do. Your ways are right and the just shall walk in them. By Your doing Jesus Christ has become to us wisdom and righteousness and sanctification and redemption. Christ our Lord is the end of the law for righteousness to all who believe (Ps 119:138; 1 Cor 1:30; Ps 48:10; Dan 9:14; Hos 14:9; Rom 10:4).

Jehovah Shammah – The Lord Is Present. Heaven is Your throne, and the earth is Your footstool. There is a house that we can build for You, for Your hand has made al these things. You have said You will dwell in us and walk among us, and be our God and we shall be Your people. So because You have said I will never leave you nor forsake you, we can say "The Lord is our Helper, we shall not be afraid of what man shall do to us." Where can I go from Your presence? If I ascend to heaven, You are there; if I make my bed in the depths, You are there (Is 66:1,2; Heb 13:5,6; Ps 139:7, 8).

Jehovah M'kaddesh – The Lord Who Sanctifies. Holy, Holy, Holy, are You, Lord of Hosts. The whole earth is full of Your glory. You are the high and lofty One that inhabits eternity. Your name is Holy. You are light and in You is no darkness at all. Holy, Holy, Holy, Lord God Almighty, who was and is, and is to come. Who shall not fear You, O Lord, and glorify Your name, for You alone are holy (Is 6:3; 57:15; 1 Jn 1:5; Rev 4:8; 15:4

You Are The Head Of All Things. Lord Jesus, You are the image of the invisible God, the first born of all creation. In You all things were created, in the heavens and on the earth. All things have been created through You and for You. You are before all things and in You all things hold together. You are the Head of the body, the Church. You are the first born from the dead – so that You Yourself might have firs place in all things. It was the Father's good pleasure for all fullness to dwell in You and through You to reconcile all things to Himself in heaven or on earth. You are the Head over all rule and authority, and in You we are made complete. Col 1:15-20;2:10.

You Are The Lamb Of God. Lord Jesus, You are the Lamb of God that takes away the sin of the world. You died for our sins according to the Scriptures. In You we have redemption through Your blood, the forgiveness of sins. Worthy is the Lamb that was slain to receive power and riches and wisdom and might and honor and glory and blessing… To Him who sits on the throne, and to the Lamb, be blessing and honor and glory forever and ever. (John 1:29; 1 Cor. 15:3; Col 1:14; Rev 5:12,13).

You Are Our Savior. Lord Jesus, You came into the world not to condemn the world but that it might be saved. There is no other name given under heaven among men whereby we might be saved. You alone are able to keep us from falling and to make us stand in the Father's presence blameless with great joy; and so to You the only God, our Savior, be glory, majesty, dominion, power, before all time, now and forever. Amen. (Jn 3:17; Acts 4:12; Jude 24,25)

You Are King of Kings. Lord Jesus, You have been exalted by God and given a Name which is above every name; that at Your name every knee should bow and every tongue shall confess that You are Lord, to the glory of God the Father. You are the blessed and only Potentate, the King of Kings and Lord of Lords. The kingdoms of this world will become Your throne, and You shall reign forever and ever. (Phil 2:9-11; 2 Tim 6:15; Rev 11:15)

You Are The Good Shepherd. Lord Jesus, You are the Good Shepherd. You know Your own, and Your own know You. You came that we might have life and have it more abundantly. You laid down Your life for us. You are the door of the sheep. Through You we enter and are safe, and go in and out and find pasture. (Jn 10:7,9,10, 11,14).

You Are The Way And The Truth. Lord Jesus, You are the Way and Truth and the life. No one can come to the Father but by You. You are the new and living way which You inaugurated for us through the veil, that is Your flesh. Through You we have access in one Spirit to the Father. You are the truth, and if You make us free, we shall be free indeed. (Jn 14:6; Heb 10:20; Eph 2:18; Jn 8:32,36)

You Are The Bread Of Life. Lord Jesus, You are the bread of life. You are the bread of God which comes down out of heaven, and gives life to the world. He who comes to You shall never hunger and he who believes in You shall never thirst. You are the One that we may eat of and not die. He who eats Your flesh and drinks Your blood has eternal life, and You will raise him up in the last day. (Jn 6:33, 35, 48, 50, 54)

You Are The Light Of The World. Lord Jesus, You are the True Light which enlightens every man coming into the world. He who follows You shall not walk in darkness, but shall have the light of life. In heaven there will be no need of the sun or the moon, for the glory of God illumines it and You are its lamp. (Jn 1:9; 8:12; Rev. 21:23).

You Are The Only Mediator. Lord Jesus, You are the only Mediator between God and man. After you made purification for our sins, You sat down at the right hand of the Majesty on high. You are able to save forever those who draw near to God through You, since You live to make intercession for us. (1 Tim 2:5; Heb 1:3; 7:25)

You Are The Resurrection And The Life. Lord Jesus, You are the resurrection and the life. The one who believes in You shall live, even if he dies; and everyone who lives and believes in You shall never die. You are the One who lives and was dead; and behold, you are alive forevermore. Amen. You have the keys of hell and death. (Jn 11:25, 26; Rev 1:18)

You Are God. You Are The Word. You were in the beginning. You were with God and You are God. He who has seen You has seen the Father. We believe You are in the Father and the Father in You. (Jn 1:1; 14:9,11)

Alpha and Omega. You are the Alpha (A) and the Omega (Z), who is and who was, and who is to come, the Almighty (Rev 1:8).

Beloved. You are the Beloved of the Father, through whom He has freely bestowed His grace (Eph 1:6).

Counselor. You are the Lord of host, whose counsel is wonderful, and whose wisdom is great. In You are held all the treasure of wisdom and knowledge (Is 28:29; Col 2:3).

Deliverer. You are the Deliverer who has come out of heaven. You are my Rock and my fortress, and my deliverer; my God, my shield, in whom I take refuge (Rom 11:26; Ps 18:2).

Immanuel. You are called Immanuel for You are God with us. He that has seen You has seen the Father (Is 7:14; Jn 14:7).

Faithful One. You are the Faithful and True One. All the promises of God in You are yes. Faithful are You who has called us, who will also do it (Rev 19:2; 2 Cor 1:20; 1 Thes. 5:24).

God Of The Whole Earth. You are our Redeemer, the Holy One of Israel, and God of the whole earth. All authority is given unto You in heaven and in earth (Is 54:5; Mt 28:18).

Head Of The Church. You are the Head of the Church, the Savior of the Body. You nourish and cherish the Church because we are members of Your body (Eph 5:23, 29. 30).

Image Of God. You are the radiance of God's glory and the exact representation of His nature; You uphold all things by the word of Your power. After You made purification of sins, you sat down at the right hand of the Majesty on high (Heb 1:3).

Grace. Your name is called Jesus for You save Your people from their sins. The law came from Moses, but grace and truth come through You (Mt 1:21; John 1).

King Of Kings. You are the blessed and only Sovereign, King of kings and Lord of Lords (1Tim 6)

Light Of The World. You are the Light of the World; he who follows You does not walk in darkness, but has the light of life (Jn 8).

Mediator. You are the only Mediator between God and man. You have become to us wisdom from God, righteousness, sanctification, and redemption (1 Tim 2:5; 1 Cor. 1).

Only Begotten. You are the only Begotten of the Father, full of grace and truth. No man has seen the Father, but You have revealed Him. You were sent to the world by Your Father's love, that whoever believes in You should not perish, but have everlasting life (Jn 1:14,18; 3:16).

Prince Of Peace. You have made it possible for us to have peace with God through justification of faith. You have made it possible for us to have peace with others through the breaking down of the middle wall of partition. You are our peace (Is 9:6; Rm 5:1; Eph 2:14).

Righteous Judge. You are the Righteous Judge. When I have fought the fight, finished the course, and kept the faith, You will give to me and to all others who have loved Your appearing the crown of righteousness (2 Tim 4:7,8).

Savior. You are the only Mediator between God and men. There is salvation in no one else; for there is not other name under heaven that has been given among men, by which we must be saved (1 Tim 2:5; Acts 4:12).

True Vine. You are the True Vine and Your Father is the Vinedresser. Every branch in You that does not bear fruit, the Father takes away, and every branch that bears fruit, He prunes it that it may bear more fruit. You are the Vine, we are the branches. If we abide in You and You abide in us, we will bear much fruit. Apart from You we can do nothing (Jn 15:1,2,5).

Pray to The Holy Spirit

One Sent. Blessed Comforter, Holy Spirit, we recognize You, acknowledge You, and Praise You as the One sent from the Father in the name of Christ to teach all things (Jn 14:26).

Comforter. Blessed Holy Spirit, we receive You as the Comforter sent from the Father to dwell with us forever (Jn 14:26)

Indweller. Indwelling Holy Spirit, who dwells in us and enables us to cry, "Abba, Father" – we praise You and will hear Your voice today (1 Cor. 3:16; Gal 4:6; Heb 3:7). Spirit of Truth, I praise You for guiding me into all truth – You have not spoken of Yourself. You have glorified Christ the Lord, and have revealed to us the deep things of God (Jn 16:13, 14; 2 Cor. 2:10).

Spreader Of The Love Of God. I praise You, Holy Spirit, for shedding abroad in our hearts the love of God which surpasses all knowledge (Rm 5:5; Eph 3:19).

Fruit Producer. I praise You and recognize You as the source of love, joy, peace, longsuffering, gentleness, godliness, faithfulness, meekness and temperance (Gal 5:22,23).

Prayer Teacher. I acknowledge You, Holy Spirit, as the One who gives us access through Jesus Christ to the Father. I praise You that You teach us to pray and that I am blessed as You pray for me and in me (Eph 2:18; Rm 8:26; Jude 20).

Re-newer. All praise to You who renews us and sanctifies us and fills us with joy (Tit 3:5; 2 Thes 2:13; 1 Thes 1:6).

Baptizer. Blessed Holy Spirit, you have baptized us into one Body in Christ, even as John the Baptist said that Christ would be the One who would baptize us in the Holy Spirit (1Cor 12:13; Mt 3:11).

Gift Giver. You are the One, blessed Spirit, who gives a variety of gifts, distributing to each one individually just as You will, giving to each one the manifestation for the common good (2 Cor 1:4, 7, 11).

Uniter and Builder. Blessed Holy Spirit, on You we are built together as the temple of God. You build us on the foundation of the apostles and prophets; Christ Jesus Himself being the chief corner stone, and in Him is the whole building being fitted together, is growing to a holy temple in the Lord (Eph 2:20-22).

Assurer. By You, Holy Spirit, we were sealed after we believed in Christ our Lord. You are the earnest of our inheritance until the redemption of this purchased possession, unto the praise of His glory (Eph 1:13,14).

Giver Of The Word. We praise You for the Word of God that came in due time, not by the will of man, but by holy men of God as they were inspired under Your moving.

Guide. We praise You that You lead us as the sons of God, and that through You we are able to mortify the deeds of the body (Rm 8:13,14).

Filler. Blessed Holy Spirit, we acknowledge You as the One who fills us with the fullness of God, and that Your presence is manifested in all goodness and righteousness and truth (Eph 5:18,19).

The One Spirit. We confess that there is one body, one Spirit, one hope of our calling, one Lord, one faith, one baptism, one God and Father of us all, who is over all, through all and in all, and that we will strive to keep Your unity in the bond of peace (Eph 4:6,7).

Only Incarnate. Blessed Spirit, we praise You that we can recognize Your presence by the confession that Jesus Christ is come in the flesh. We will not believe every spirit, but test them to see if they are from God (1 Jn 4:2,3)

Convicting. Blessed Holy Spirit, You are the one who convicts the world of sin, righteousness and judgment. Of sin, because they believe not in Christ; of righteousness, because He has gone to the Father and we see Him no more; and of judgment, because the prince of this world is judged. You will indeed guide us into all the truth (Jn 16:8-13).

Conducting Man-to-Man Ministry

How to Do Individual Disciple Making by Jack Griffith

Before we actually look at what man to man is, let me give you four verses to show that man to man is not just a Navigator idea, but rather a New Testament method of training and teaching.

1. "Even though you have ten thousand guardians in Christ, you do not have many fathers, for in Christ Jesus I became your father through the gospel." (1 Corinthians 4:15)

2. "For you know that we dealt with each of you as a father deals with his own children, encouraging, comforting and urging you to live lives worthy of God, who calls you into his kingdom and glory." (1 Thessalonians 2:11, 12)

3. "So be on your guard! Remember that for three years I never stopped warning each of you night and day with tears." (Acts 20:31)

4. "And the things you have heard me say in the presence of many witnesses entrust to reliable men who will also be qualified to teach others." (2 Timothy 2:2)

What is man to man?

It is meeting another, individually eyeball to eyeball, face to face. It involves sharing your whole life and ministry with him, so he, by the grace of God, will progress from spiritual immaturity to spiritual maturity in Christ. "We loved you so much that we were delighted to share with you not only the gospel of God but our lives as well, because you had become so dear to us." (1 Thessalonians 2:8). "...until we all reach unity in the faith and in the knowledge of the Son of God and become mature, attaining to the whole measure of the fullness of Christ." (Ephesians 4:13).

The question is often asked, "What is the difference between follow up and man-to-man?" It's as if follow up is a shotgun ministry, often by groups and extensive in design. Man To Man is the rifle, working one at a time and intensive in its aim.

Follow up is a spiritual nursery involving groups and some individual attention, but man to man is personal to faithful men (2 Timothy 2:2). A faithful man is one who is dependable, reliable, and trustworthy. When you suggest he do something, he does it. The testimony of Joshua is that he was this kind of faithful man. "As the LORD commanded his servant Moses, so Moses commanded Joshua, and Joshua did it; he left nothing undone of all that the LORD commanded Moses." (Joshua 11:15). To test his desire and faithfulness, give him something to do – perhaps a simple assignment. Luke 16:10 says "Whoever can be trusted with very little can also be trusted with much, and whoever is dishonest with very little will also be dishonest with much."

A book that has been of great help is "Disciples Are Made Not Born", by Walt Henrichsen, who until 1978 was on staff with the Navigators. Chapter one is entitled, "The type of man God uses" and in it he lists nine features in the life of a faithful man.

1. He has adopted as his objective in life the same objective God sets forth in the Scriptures. (Matthew 6:33) – to see God's kingdom and righteousness as the first priority.
2. He is willing to pay any price to have the will of God fulfilled in his life (2 Timothy 2:3, 4).
3. He as a love for the Word of God (Jeremiah 15:16).
4. He has a servant heart (Matthew 20:26-28).
5. He has no confidence in the flesh (Romans 7:18).
6. He does not have an independent spirit (2 Corinthians 3:5).
7. He has a love for people (1 John 4:11).
8. He does not allow himself to be trapped in bitterness (Hebrews 12:15).
9. He has learned to discipline his life (1 Corinthians 9:24-47).

Is your man willing to measure up to these things – to be developing them? If not, then you are investing your life into an unfaithful man and Proverbs 25:19 says, "Like a bad tooth or a lame foot is reliance on the unfaithful in times of trouble."

How do we start meeting on a man-to-man basis?

1. Pray for a hungry, thirsty hearted man to work with – just as Jesus Himself sought out the thirsty ones. In the last day, that great *day* of the feast, Jesus stood and cried, saying, If any man thirst, let him come unto me, and drink (John 7:37).

2. Remember that it is God that gives us men. "I have revealed you to those whom you gave me out of the world. They were yours; you gave them to me and they have obeyed your word. ...I pray for them. I am not praying for the world, but for those you have given me, for they are yours (John 17:6, 9). "Saul also went to his home in Gibeah, accompanied by valiant men whose hearts God had touched (1 Samuel 10:26). See also Numbers 27:15-20 regarding Moses and Joshua. For many years I believed Moses chose Joshua as his

replacement. Not so. Joshua was chosen by God. Begin praying, "Lord, You choose the one in whom I am to invest my life."

3. Be alert to the ones growing faster than others in bible study groups.

4. Got to them – one, or at most two. Ask if they would like to meet with you on a personal man-to-man level for special, intensive training.

5. Explain to them what the cost will be in time, priorities and discipline and ask them to pray about it. When I was setting up a training program for laymen in churches eight years ago, it was known that I was looking for some faithful men to be on the training program team. If anyone was interested, they were to see me within the next few weeks. I was simply praying, "Lord, give me a handful of men that are Your choice." Five men came. I laid down the qualifications. A high standard was necessary. All five went home to pray and all five came back to take up the challenge of being team leaders on the Shamgar training program. Play a man's game, a man's way and you'll get men! Play a boy's game and you'll get boys.

6. If they are still interested, explain the 2 Timothy 2:2 principle and the nine features of a faithful man. If he is willing to come to this standard and if he has a willing and teachable heart, I would suggest you start with him.

7. Set a day and time to start. Either once a week or twice a month is best. If the Shamgar program the family commitments of the team leaders mean that twice a month is best.

8. Have a trial of two to three months then both of you evaluate the worth of continuing or making some changes. It took me a long time to find that faithful man I had been challenged to pray for; so be patient, but hit for that faithful one. Remember, he is more than a faithful man – he is a "faithful man who shall be able to teach others also…" Don't feel you are too young in the Lord – a pace setter has only to be one step ahead.

   What are you trying to teach him? All that your spiritual father taught you. Every Christian needs to ask himself two questions: 1) Who is my Paul? 2) Who is my Timothy? (i.e. Who am I helping to become a fruitful disciple maker?)

Practical hints in man-to-man

1. Make sure you are well prepared. Pray and organize before you spend time with a man. Remember you will produce after your own kind. If you are faithful in your daily, early morning quiet time – seven minutes, seven mornings a week before breakfast – that's the type of man you're going to produce. If you're weak, then that is the type of man you will produce. If you are a fanatic on scripture memory – you'll produce another fanatic! If scripture memory means nothing to you, it will mean nothing to him. You will teach by

your life. More is caught than is taught. The same goes for all the other basic disciplines of the Christian life.

2. Aim at winning his heart. Proverbs 27:19 says "As water reflects a face, so a man's heart reflects the man." Pray before he comes, "Lord, give me Joe's heart when he comes tonight."

3. Remember that you can't lead anyone further than you have gone. You cannot lay solid foundations in other lives from what are only sketchy outlines in your own.

4. You teach by the example of your own life. Paul said this very thing in Philippians 4:9, "Whatever you have learned or received or heard from me, or seen in me – put it into practice. And the God of peace will be with you." The person who is ministering man to man, must be what he is trying to teach. To repeat what I said earlier, the learner will sooner follow the example of his teacher than he will his word.

5. In man to man take nothing for granted. When you are beginning with a man and he tells you something, whatever it is check, check and double check it! Your not doubting his word, you are just taking nothing for granted.

6. Repeat all things. Both you to him and him to you. "He tells us everything over and over again, a line at a time and in such simple words." (Isaiah 28:10 Living). John Ridgeway and some other young men at the university of NSW, in the early days of the Australian Navigator work, remember well this principle. I would have man to man with John and Graham French and afterwards they would ask one another, "What did he give you today?" – "He gave me the same thing he's been giving me for the past couple of months!" Recently, before 1,100 people, John said how glad he was that I went over them again and again and again. "Because" he said, "They became a part of my life." Make no apologies for repeating things. Get him to write down what you have said and after he as written it, get him to read it back to you. Often you will detect at this point that here has not been 100% comprehension of you what you have said.

7. Give him attainable assignments. Proverbs 13:19, "A longing fulfilled is sweet to the soul, but fools detest turning from evil." If you happen to be shoveling all you have into this man – please, burn your shovel! Get out the eye dropper or the thimble. You will find you get more mileage out of "Line upon line, line upon line; here a little, and there a little…(Isaiah 28:10). I have what I cal the drip system. Let me explain. Thirty years ago my wife, May and I built a home in Haberfield, just outside of the city of Sydney. At the gateway we planned two lovely pine trees. I didn't have time to water them; I was a busy businessman in those days. (When I came to Christ I became a busy Christian instead). For thirty years I let the Lord water those pine trees. As I come out the door, on the left side of the gate is a tree about six meters tall and four meters wide – boy it's alive! Just over one meter away, is another pine tree, planted at the same time. Its only two meters high and about one meter wide – it doesn't look so well.

Why? The big one happens to have a tap at its base. For thirty years I have been unable to stop the slow drip that's been there. I've had plumber after plumber – but still there's a slow drip. Just try the slow drip method. Seven minutes with God, seven days a week before breakfast. In time seven will become fourteen, then maybe twenty eight.

8. Take him with you as much as possible. Take him witnessing with you, take him if you have a church assignment whenever you can, take him with you. This is what Jesus did with His disciples – as He taught them, He took them with Him. "He appointed twelve – designating them apostles – that they might be with Him and that He might send them out to preach." (Mark 3:14).

9. Inspect him as well as expect of him. If you give him something to do, expect him to do it, but when he comes to see you next time, inspect him to make sure he has done it. He in turn will realize your interest in him and in the future will strive to do well.

10. Use as many pass-on-able illustrations as possible. Make sure he gets it through the eye gate as well as the ear gate. Use such illustrations as the Wheel, the Word hand, the Prayer hand, and the Bridge. The Chinese proverbs is right, "One picture is worth a thousand words." I don't' know about you, but what I see sinks in faster than what I hear.

11. Share your whole life with him. Share your weaknesses as well as your strengths. Allow yourself to be transparent before him. I was speaking in Brisbane some time back on the subject of scripture memory. I explained how motivated I was on scripture memory, but at the same time was revealing how hard I had to work to keep learning a verse myself. I had to explain that if it took them twenty times through a verse to learn it, it would take me forty. But I am motivated because I know the value of scripture memory.

    One of the key men there came to me later and said that it had been a real blessing to hear that I labored hard at scripture memory. "I have so much trouble myself", he said, "but if you can keep at it there's no reason why I should be discouraged." Remember to be open with your man.

12. Share with him as a friend – not a teacher / pupil attitude. Always be enthusiastic about all the things you share with him. Be an encourager to him at every opportunity. "…each helps the other and says to his brother, "be strong!" The craftsman encourages the goldsmith, and he who smoothes with the hammer spurs on him who strikes the anvil." (Isaiah 41:6, 7). The lowly carpenter was an encouragement to the upper class goldsmith. In the early days of the Navigator work, here I was with limited education, doing man to man with two pastors and five university students. Praise the Lord that He does the work through us.

13. In everything show him how. We are long in telling people what to do, but we are short in show them how.

14. Tailor your program to meet the need of the individual. Why? Because each one is different. Don't try to pour them al into the one mold.

15. Keep sharing the Lordship of Christ. "Today in the town of David a Savior has been born to you; He is Christ the Lord." (Luke 2:11). "If anyone comes to me and does not hate his father and mother, his wife and children, his brothers and sisters – yes, even his own life – he cannot be my disciple. And anyone who does not carry his cross and follow me cannot be my disciple." (Luke 14:26, 27). 'In the same way, any of you who does not give up everything he has cannot be my disciple." (Luke 14:33).

16. Five things to remember.
    a. Tell him why – it is important.
    b. Show him how – the way to do it.
    c. Get him started – with specific suggestions.
    d. Keep him going – by visits or phone calls.
    e. Get him to reproduce all this in another life (2 Timothy 2:2).

17. Help him to establish his goals in life. For example, to know Christ and to make him known (Philippians 3:10), Colossians 1:27-29). To know Christ is the vertical aspects of the wheel – to make him known represents the horizontal spokes.

18. Remember Psalm 127:1 "Unless the Lord builds the house, its builders labor in vain. Unless the Lord watches over the city, the watchman stand guard in vain." (1 Corinthians 3:6, 7) "I planted the seed, Apollos watered it but God made it grow. So neither he who plants nor he who waters is anything, but only God who makes things grow." (Philippians 2:13) "for it is God who works in you to will and to act according to his good pleasure." Lets not forget, it is God who is the Master Trainer – He builds the man.

Suggested man-to-man session

This is simply a skeleton outline; you will have to take this and adapt it to suit your particular situation. You can add or subtract from it.

1. Always pray before he comes for the meeting together. Perhaps you could pray Exodus 4:12, "Now go; I will help you speak and will teach you what to say."

2. Have him visit you if possible. You may be very busy in ministry and therefore you will not have the time to travel from place to place. It will challenge him to pursue help. It is granted that this is not always possible

3. Always greet him with a warm handshake and smile. This is a simple little thing that unfortunately doesn't always happen. Make him feel welcome.

4. If night time, leave the front light turned on. Leave the hall light on too – this will assure him he is expected.

5. Always aim for punctuality. "But everything should be done in a fitting and orderly way." (1 Corinthians 14:40). If you are going to meet him a 8:00 o'clock, say "Joe its 7:50 am for a 8:00 am start." This is the way it is in the Shamgar team meetings and man to man sessions. In the army the 9:00 am parade wasn't at 9:01! Much would happen if you were be one minute late for a parade. Should we expect less in our Christian life? Also, for the end of your time together, make sure you finish on time. Start promptly and finish promptly at a pre-arranged time. On the team, we meet with fellows twice a month for 1 to 1 ½ hours. You may prefer once a week – find out what suits you and the man you're meeting.

6. Always be neatly dressed. This is not suggesting that a coat and tie is necessary, just that you are tidy. Make sure your meeting place is tidy – comfortable and uncluttered. Sit opposite one another rather than alongside each other. This ensures eye contact. It is very important to catch him eyeball to eyeball.

7. First, have a friendly chat. If you visit him greet his family. Let him tell you about his studies or work etc. and be a good listener. "Set a guard over my mouth O Lord; keep watch over the door of my lips." (Psalm 141:3). For a little while let him do the talking. Another verse that is helpful is James 1:19 "My dear brothers, take note of this: Everyone should be quick to listen, slow to speak and slow to become angry." God has given us two ears and one mouth. Lets be twice as long on hearing as we are on speaking.

8. You always open in prayer. If he is a new man, a young fellow in the Lord, just a short sentence will do.

9. If meeting for the first time, check him on his assurance of salvation. Make sure he has a Bible based assurance. If he has no assurance, let me give you three verses God has used in my own life and ministry (John 1:12; Romans 10;9, 10; 1 John 5:11, 12). The reason you must be sure of his salvation, is frankly that it is a useless exercise unless he is born again by the Spirit of God – you can't feed a dead baby! Make sure this is the first step. Another Chinese proverb says, "To commence the journey of 1000 miles, you must take the first step." Those three verses are handy to have dated in your Bible with the day you invited Jesus Christ to come into your life. If your man sees the dates he will inquire, you will explain what it means and he'll do exactly the same. May and I came to Christ at the same time on the same day and dated verses in our Bibles, April 12th 1959.

10. Exchange blessings since you last met. Some evidences of God's hand, His guidance, or blessings from your time alone with the Lord.

11. Proceed to check him on his daily disciplines and priorities. Check his assignments for the previous one or two weeks. "How have you been doing in your quiet times in the past two weeks?" "Have you made it seven out of seven before breakfast?" Remind him

if he fails that the victory at 6:00 am is won a 10:00 pm the night before. It may cost you – you may miss the England / Scotland replay or the Wimbledon final, but a disciple of Jesus Christ is a revolutionary. On the Shamgar team we encourage men to make a covenant with the Lord "For me Lord from now on – no Bible, no breakfast1" Job 23:12 says, "I have not departed from the commands of his lips; I have treasured the words of his mouth more than my daily bread." Jesus set the example of rising early to meet the Father, "Very early in the morning, while it was still dark, Jesus got up, left the house and went off to a solitary place where he prayed." (Mark 1:35). Some of disciplines and priorities of the Shamgar team check:

    a. Daily quiet times
    b. Daily Bible reading calendar – a short, written application from the reading is recorded on one or two lines of 3x5 card.
    c. Scripture Memory – Check their last few weeks of review, current verses and if they have finished the TMS (Topical Memory System) we go through the outline.
    d. Bible Study – check particularly the application questions.
    e. Witnessing Opportunities – are they praying daily for the chance to speak to someone today about Jesus Christ? Does he carry a couple of tracks in his pocket? Is his testimony sharp?

12. Keep sharing with him the vision of disciple making (Matthew 28:18-20). Be a disciple – make disciples – develop disciple makers. Don't forget you must be one before you can make one.

13. Always keep the basics of the Christian life in focus. Major on Christ the center. 1 Corinthians 3:11 says that Christ is the only foundation on which to build. "For no one can lay any foundation other than the one already laid, which is Christ Jesus."

14. Keep 2 Timothy 2:2 before him. "Joe, how is your Timothy doing?" "Joe. Have you thought about praying for a faithful man – a Timothy to invest in?" Concentrate on faithful men, who will able to teach others also. (Paul also spent time with other faithful men – Titus, Silas, etc.) Jesus spent most of His time with twelve men during a continuous period of three years and devoted particular attention to three of these men (Peter, James and John). These men were later to become the pillars of the church (Galatians 2:9). Quality produces quantity – quantity itself does not produce quality. As intensive ministry will produce extensive ministry. Give your life to a few, who in turn will multiply into many.

15. Always keep sharing with him the importance of the basics in his life. This is found in the Wheel illustration.

16. Meet his needs through the Word if possible. Question him. Find out if there is anything he would want you to pray through with him. Is there something he wants to share confidentially.

17. Give him attainable assignments each meeting. I know I repeat myself but its important that there is some personal investigation. Both of you write down the assignment.

18. Get him to share any new promises from the Word he is claiming.

19. Finish on time and have him close in a brief word of prayer.

20. Confirm the date and time of your next meeting. Again, both of you write it down.

21. Thank him for his fellowship. Share with him Proverbs 11:25 "A generous man will prosper; he who refreshes others will himself be refreshed." "Joe, thanks for the time tonight, it has been a real blessing to me." This is simply a word of encouragement.

22. See him off with a warm smile and a hand shake.

23. Go to your prayer closet and thank God for the time together.

Facilitating a Men's Bible Study

Introduction

The purpose of this handout is to provide a basic framework for men's ministry Bible study discussions. Using this guide will help stimulate good discussion and mutual sharing among the men who participate in study group meetings. Being a good facilitator is not difficult; however, to have a quality group discussion will take time, forethought, and effort. The more a facilitator works at improving his techniques, the more rewarding the content of his group discussions. *Keep in mind; it is all about the men across the table.*

Discuss Topics Using a Question and Answer Format

For each session, the facilitator uses a set of questions to begin a discourse among the men in a group. The questions aim at getting the men feeling comfortable and lead into deeper conversation.

Here is an example from a typical first session:

1. Be sure everyone in the group is introduced to one another
2. Q – Why did you choose to join a study like this one?
3. Q – What expectations do you personally have here at the beginning?
4. Q – What part of this study impressed you most?
5. Q – Why do feel that way?
6. Suggestion for Next Session: A 3 ring bind would be helpful to keep all your study handouts in one place.

During the discourse, there will be opportunities to help stimulate the conversation. Some men will need to be encouraged to open up and participate in the discussion; others will want to start conversing immediately. A major responsibility for a facilitator is to ensure that all men have an equal opportunity to participate and share.

Questions are a great way to stimulate and guide a group discussion. Man-to-Man ministry recommends using five question types: approach, observation, interpretation, application, and extenders. Understanding how to use these types of questions enables a facilitator to guide, stimulate, and monitor the discussions of men.

Ask Good Questions

The primary purpose for asking oral questions is to stimulate the participants to think and enter into a meaningful dialog.

Approach questions get the men thinking about the topic

- On a scale of one to ten, one being low and ten being high, what is your level of understanding biblical manhood?
- By show of hands, how many of you pray privately on a regular basis?
- Have you ever considered how your manhood appears to others?

Observation questions reveal the content of the topic

- What are some specific things God knows about you?
- What did you learn from this presentation?
- How does a person _____.
- What are the four faces of manhood?

Interpretation questions help determine what the author meant

- What is meant by the word _____?
- What does it mean that God knew David?
- What does unconditional love mean?
- What does it mean that God is Father?
- Why do you think Robert said _____.
- Why do you think Jesus died on the cross?
- Why do you feel Jesus should be Lord of your life?
- Why is it important for men to understand godly manhood?
- Why do you need to have a right relationship with your earthly father?

Application questions help put the topic into actual practice

- What can you do to better glorify God as man?

- How can you benefit from God's complete knowledge of you?
- How do you receive this love from God?
- What assurance do you have that you are part of God's family?
- What are you going to do as a result from studying this text?
- How does this verse make a difference in the life of a godly man?
- How can you apply this truth to your daily life?

Discussion extenders keep the dialog moving

The discussion can be enhanced and kept moving by short, guiding questions. They fall into six categories: extending, clarifying, justifying, redirecting, fact, and feeling.

Extending

- What else can you add to that?
- What else did you notice?
- What else did the rest of you discover?
- Could you explain that more fully?
- Do you have any more thoughts on that?
- Would you like to add anything else?

Clarifying

- What do you mean by that?
- Could you rephrase that statement?

Justifying

- Would you explain that?
- What reason can you give for that?

Redirecting

- Jay, what do you think?
- What did you notice Dan?

Fact (a focused Observation question)

- What are two things he stressed?
- What is the main point he covered?
- What are the steps to leading a person to Christ?
- What is the purpose of evangelism?

Feeling

- How did you react to his main point?
- How do you feel when sharing your personal testimony?
- Why do you feel this is true?
- Why is it important to discuss godly manhood?
- Why does God allow suffering?

Exercise Sound Principles for Men's Study Groups

The following do's and don'ts are taken from "Effective Men's Ministry" a book produced by the National Coalition of Men's Ministries.

Do

Concentrate

The key to establishing effective communication in a group is good listening. Without good listening skills, there is no group. Look at the man who is speaking, don't interrupt, and don't be distracted by thinking about what you are going to say next – listen and learn.

Facilitate

Keep the conversation uplifting and progressive in growth. Make sure the discussion questions are open-ended and require more than a yes, no or maybe response. Be sure that you leave enough time for everyone to be involved.

Punctuate

Stick to the time allowed for your group meetings. Start and end on time. Tardiness or consistently running over the allotted time will kill a group before long. Make your group a priority and stay within the time parameters.

Imitate Jesus

Demonstrate grace, acceptance, understanding, compassion, and unconditional love of Christ to the members of your group.

Participate

If the group is to succeed, everyone must be involved. This involvement includes opening one's life honestly before others. [1]

Don't

Dominate

Do not allow one or two men in your group to dominate the conversation or group discussion. Hogging the stage causes others to withdraw or not interact with the group, and these men will soon become disinterested spectators. The way of group domination is not the avenue for growth.

Intimidate

Avoid intimidation at all costs. Some men in your group will be insecure. Others will have been intimidated most of their lives due to physical size, wealth, appearance, family, job, or how long they have been a Christian. Until you know where everyone in the group stands, be careful about going too deep or assuming that al members know all the Christian terms and their meanings

Humiliate

Some men belittle others in order to appear funny or secure. This habit of sarcasm or cutting remarks will undermine trust and intimacy in a group. If one person is picked on in jest by another and other people laugh, he might sense that everyone is ganging up on him.

Interrogate

Most men will not open up when faced with a battery of questions that appear confrontational or "in your face." Though shooting straight is the best way to approach a group, grace is still a vital characteristic of a Christ like attitude.

Fabricate

To gain the most from a group study, all members must be honest with one another. The truthfulness of answers will depend greatly on the group's commitment to confidentiality.

---

[1] Geoff Gorsuch, <u>Effective Men's Ministry</u>, (Grand Rapids, MI: Zondervan, 2001) p. 155.

Agitate

Not everyone has a great day every day. Coming to a group study and being confronted with personal shortcomings may not be pleasant. Treat one another with patience, grace, and gentleness.

Procrastinate

Follow up on action points within the group, to make sure everyone is making time to grow in their commitments. If a brother stumbles, the others should pick him up and carry him, if necessary.

Hesitate

When a man in your group has a definite need, don't just say you will pray. Write it down and make it the first item during time for prayer! If he has a physical need, pitch in and help him out. [2]

Capitulate

Never give up on the members of your group study. Sometimes it may appear there is little or no change in a man's behavior, when in reality God's is working. "Let us not lose heart in doing good, for in due time we will reap if we do not grow weary" (Galatians 6:9).

---

[2] Ibid., p. 153.

Handle Difficult Men with Tact

Men can sometimes be difficult to keep on track and may need extra help in being a "one another" member of a group study. Here are several suggestions to help you deal with possible disruptions:

- Never put down a disruptive man. Try to make a positive comment, while at the same time asking for a change in behavior. Deal with the problem early before it takes the course and the class off-track.

- If the participant talks too much ask the rest of the group:
  - "What does anyone else think about this point?"
  - "Who else has some ideas?"
  - "Let's make sure everyone gets a chance to contribute before any one person speaks twice."

- If the participant talks too long, wait for a pause and interrupt. Say, "Could you please summarize your idea in a few words? Our time is very limited."

- If the man talks to someone else at length, say, "Pardon me, John. We can't hear what you and Sam are saying. Would you mind sharing it with all of us?"

- If a man challenges your ideas or opinions:

  - Cite your information source(s). Acknowledge that other sources (name if possible) think otherwise.

  - Ask the group what they think about the challenger's opinion.

  - Acknowledge that the challenger's opinion has merit and that you may need to do some rethinking.

Keep in mind love covers a multitude of sins. All of us are in process. The men in a group study are there because they sense a need to grow as men. God is in the business of changing men's lives. It is why were all in this together!

Should a difficult situation occur, contact the sponsor, and solicit whatever assistance you need to resolve the conflict.

"May the God of peace, who through the blood of the eternal covenant brought back from the dead our Lord Jesus, that great Shepherd of the sheep, equip you with everything good for doing His will, and me He work in us what is pleasing to Him, through Jesus Christ, to whom be glory for ever and ever. Amen." (Hebrews 13:20-21).

Be a One Another Brother

The New Testament lists numerous verses describing how brothers in the church are to treat one another. Below are twenty-five distinct ways men can live as brothers in Christ.

1. Love One Another – John 13:34-35
2. Greet One Another – Romans 16:16
3. Accept One Another – Romans 15:7
4. Be Devoted to One Another – Romans 12:10
5. Live In Harmony with One Another – Romans 12:16
6. Stop Judging One Another – Romans 14:13
7. Instruct One Another – Romans 15:14
8. Encourage One Another – 1 Thessalonians 5:11
9. Build Up One Another – 1 Thessalonians 5:11
10. Confess Sins to One Another – James 5:16
11. Pray for One Another – James 5:16
12. Agree With One Another – 1 Corinthians 1:10
13. Serve One Another - Galatians 5:13
14. Carry One Another's Burdens – Galatians 6:2
15. Be Patient with One Another - Ephesians 4:2
16. Be Compassionate to One Another – Ephesians 4:32
17. Speak Properly to One Another – Ephesians 5:19
18. Submit to One Another – Ephesians 5:21
19. Forgive One Another – Colossians 3:13
20. Admonish One Another – Colossians 3:16
21. Spur One Another – Hebrews 10:24-25
22. Do Not Slander One Another – James 4:11
23. Offer Hospitality to One Another – 1 Peter 4:9
24. Demonstrate Humility to One Another – 1 Peter 5:5
25. Fellowship with One Another – 1 John 1:7

Part IV - Appendices

Appendix A – Men's Ministry Job Roles and Descriptions

This is a recommended set of MM roles and descriptions to form and grow your ministry team. Each church and men's ministry team has unique needs and may not use all of them or some leaders assign multiple roles to one or two men. The Iron Sharpens Iron network recommends the following positions based on church size.

Men's Ministry Team Structure (Church of 75-200)

- *Team Leader (chairperson/Captain/etc)* - This is the man with a clear vision for ministry to and through men and who has 'a hearing' with the men of the church. He is the 'upfront' guy who is liked and respected by the majority of the congregation. He is also willing and able to take on some of the administrative work of the men's ministry.

- *Pastor* - Close to half the adults in the church are men so he needs to be part of this team. His role on the team is to listen and sometimes advise. His role outside of the team is to 'champion' men's ministry to the congregation. Everyone in the church should know that ministry to and through men is one of his most important priorities.

- *Event Leader* - This man sees events he as part of the men's ministry big picture. He is careful to schedule everything so that it complements the overall ministry of the local church. He is also looking for opportunities to take part in regional events and resources.

- *Disciple Maker and Small Groups Leader* - This is a man who has a passion to see the men get connected. His role is to match up as many men as are willing with a small group or with someone that can disciple them. He may oversee some type of formal mentoring program. He has resources for small group leaders and serves as a coach to these leaders.

Men's Ministry Team Structure (Church of 200-500)

- *Team Leader (Champion)* - This is the man with a clear vision for ministry to and through men and who has 'a hearing' with the men of the church. He is the 'upfront' guy who is liked and respected by the majority of the congregation.

- *Senior Pastor.* Close to half the adults in the church are men so he needs to be part of this team. His role on the team is to listen and sometimes advise. His role outside of the team is to 'champion' men's ministry to the congregation. Everyone in the church should know that ministry to and through men is one of his most important priorities.

\ *Associate Pastor* (adult ministries/discipleship/etc) This is the staff person with the responsibility to oversee ministry to men. He helps develop a budget for the men's ministry. He shepherds and sometimes disciples the men on the leadership team. He makes sure that men's ministry is integrated into the life and ministry of the church.

\ *Prayer Leader.* This man mobilizes men for prayer. He organizes at least one team of men to pray with and for the pastor.

\ *Event Leader.* This man sees events he as part of the men's ministry big picture. He is careful to schedule everything so that it complements the overall ministry of the local church. He is also looking for opportunities to take part in regional events and resources.

\ *Discipling and Small Groups Leader.* This is a man who has a passion to see the men get connected. His role is to match up as many men as are willing with a small group or with someone that can disciple them. He may oversee some type of formal mentoring program. He has resources for small group leaders and serves as a coach to these leaders.

\ *Administrative Leader.* This is the man on the team who handles the mailings and sign-ups. The database would be his responsibility.

Men's Ministry Team Structure (Church of 500+)

\ *Team Leader (Champion)* - This is the man with a clear vision for ministry to and through men and who has 'a hearing' with the men of the church. He is the 'upfront' guy who is liked and respected by the majority of the congregation.

\ *Senior Pastor* - Close to half the adults in the church are men so he needs to be part of this team. His role on the team is to attend a team meeting at least once each year. He will listen and sometimes advise. His role outside of the team is to 'champion' men's ministry to the congregation. Everyone in the church should know that ministry to and through men is one of his most important priorities.

\ *Associate Pastor (adult ministries/discipleship)* - This is the staff person with the responsibility to oversee ministry to men. He helps develop a budget for the men's ministry. He shepherds and sometimes disciples the men on the leadership team. He makes sure that men's ministry is integrated into the life and ministry of the church.

\ *Prayer Leader.* This man is not just an intercessor, but a trainer and a creative mobilizer of men for prayer. He has administrative skills that allow him to organize a prayer chain/tree. His greatest strength is his burden to 'see men pray' in his local church. He champions any event that brings a man to the throne.

\ *Event Leaders (3-4).* These men take on one event per year so that they do not burn out. They are team leaders and recruiters. Each man sees the event he is responsible for as part of the men's ministry big picture. They are careful to complement their labors and not compete with each other's events.

\ *Disciple Making Leader.* This is a man who has been personally discipled and who is discipling others. His role is to match up as many men as are willing with someone that can disciple them. He may oversee some type of formal mentoring program.

\ *Small Groups Leader.* This is a man who has been blessed by his small group and wants the same experience for every man in his church. He is relational and is organized. His role is to know who is in a men's small group and who is not. He gives ongoing encouragement to the small group leaders. He is the small group champion.

\ *Outreach Leader.* This man is gifted in evangelism and passionate for the lost. He understands masculine context and has many creative ideas of how to connect to and reach lost men. He has some training skills and takes responsibility to equip men to share their personal story as well as the gospel story. He may work with the event leaders on developing an outreach event.

\ *Administrative Leader.* This is the man on the team who handles the mailings and sign-ups. The database would be his responsibility. He is creative and enjoys making posters and brochures and going to Kinko's! He would oversee a 'call team' that gives the men of the church a personal invite to events.

Appendix B - Men's Ministry Leadership Team Commitment

Use this document as a means for securing one year commitments from our mm leadership team

Leadership Attributes:

- ☐ Spend one year consistently participating in men's ministry (i.e. monthly men's breakfast)
- ☐ Strive to consistently grow in their walk with God (not perfection, but honestly making a consistent effort)
- ☐ Seek a serving position of responsibility (serve on breakfast crew, facilitate a small group, or organize an event)
- ☐ Demonstrate faithfulness while serving in that position
- ☐ If married, maintain consistent growth and effort to love wife as Christ loved the church

Team Selection Process:

- ☐ Each year prior to the leadership summit, the current team members will evaluate a list of individuals who have demonstrated the minimum leadership attributes as listed above
- ☐ After prayerfully evaluating each man based on the leadership attributes as outlined above, selected individuals will be
  - contacted and invited to the annual leadership summit
  - asked to serve one year on the leadership team
- ☐ Each team member will have a specific role with assigned responsibilities
- ☐ All men answering yes to this call to serve will be given a copy of this covenant to pray over and sign as God leads them to do so

Men's Ministry Leadership Team Expectations – I commit to:

- ☐ maintain the minimum leadership attributes as outlined above
- ☐ complete a basic discipleship training course if I have not already done so
- ☐ pray for God to give me a man to disciple
- ☐ seek to be held and to hold others accountable to live as godly men
- ☐ deepen my personal relationship with God
- ☐ develop my brotherhood with other men
- ☐ strive to live as a mature disciple of Jesus Christ
- ☐ renew my commitment each year or move into another area of ministry in the church*

I have prayed over the contents of this covenant and am ready to covenant with the other members of the leadership team to serve God through this ministry.

Signature: _____Date: _____

* During the course of ministry it is normal for men to sense God call them to other areas of ministry. This will allow for God to redirect individuals to other areas in the church should the Holy Spirit set them apart for different works of ministry. If you have done your job, these men will be **sent out** rather than leave. At the end of the year be sure to celebrate with every member of the team. We serve an awesome God!

Appendix C - Recommended List of Men's Ministry Resources

The following resources are recommended tools to help you as you lead your men and disciple them for a life of kingdom service.

Strategy
- Brad Stewart, *Teams and Teamwork* (San Bernadino, CA: Create Space) 2016
- Phil Downer *Effective Men's Ministry* (Grand Rapids, MI: Zondervan, 2001)
- Morley, Delk, & Clemmer, *No Man Left Behind* (Chicago, IL: Moody Press, 2006)
- Steve Sonderman, *How to Build a Life Changing Men's Ministry* (Minneapolis, MN: Bethany House 1996)
- Brad Lewis, *Men's Ministry in the 21st Century* (Loveland, CO: Group Publishing, 2004)

Godly Masculinity
- John Eldredge, *Wild at Heart* (Nashville, TN: Thomas Nelson, 2001)
- John Eldredge, *The Way of the Wild Heart* (Nashville, TN: Thomas Nelson, 2006)
- Dave Murrow, *Why Men Hate Going to Church* (Nashville, TN: Thomas Nelson, 2005)
- Paul Coughlin, *No More Christian Nice Guy* (Minneapolis, MN: Bethany House, 2005)
- Mark Galli, *Jesus Mean and Wild* (Grand Rapids, MI: Baker Books, 2006)

Small Groups
- Geoff Gorsuch, Brothers! *Calling Men into Vital Relationships* (Colorado Springs, CO: Navpress, 1994)
- Jimmy Long, *Small Group Leaders Handbook* (Downers Grove, IL: InterVarsity Press, 1995)

Mentoring
- Stanley & Clinton, *Connecting* (Colorado Springs, CO: Navpress, 1992)
- Hendricks & Hendricks, *As Iron Sharpens Iron* (Chicago, IL: Moody Press, 1995)

Servant Leadership
- Patrick Morley, *Pastoring Men* (Chicago, IL: Moody Publishers, 2009)
- Blackaby, *Called to Be God's Leader* (Nashville, TN: Thomas Nelson, 2004)
- J. Oswald Sanders, *Spiritual Leadership* (Chicago, IL: Moody Press, 1967)
- Bobby Welch, *The Warrior Leader* (Nashville, TN: Broadman & Holman Publishers, 2004)

Men's Issues
- Pat Morley, *Man In The Mirror* (Grand Rapids, MI: Zondervan, 1989)
- Robert Lewis, *The Quest for Authentic Manhood* (Men's Fraternity – DVD Series, 800-446-7228 www.men'sfraternity.com)
- Bob Buford, *Half Time* (Grand Rapids, MI: Zondervan, 1997)
- Steve Farrar, *Point Man* (Portland, OR: Multnomah Books, 1990)
- Stephen Arterburn, *The Secrets Men Keep* (Nashville, TN: Integrity Publishers, 2006)
- Doug Sherman and William Hendricks, *Your Work Matters to God* (Colorado Springs, CO: Navpress, 1987)

Lust and Sexual Temptations
- Stephen Arterburn & Fred Stoeker, *Every Man's Battle* (Colorado Springs, CO: Waterbook Press, 2000

Spiritual Warfare
- Stu Weber, *Spirit Warrior* (Portland, OR: Multnomah Books, 2001)
- Chip Ingram, *The Invisible War* (Grand Rapids, MI: Baker Books, 2006)

Discipleship Books and Programs
- Bill Hull, *The Complete Book of Discipleship*, (Colorado Springs, CO: NavPress, 2006)
- Walter A. Henrichsen, *Disciples Are Made Not Born* (Wheaton, Ill.: Victor Books, 2002)
- Leroy Eims, *The Lost Art of Disciple Making* (Grand Rapids, MI: Zondervan, 1978
- CBMC, *Operation Timothy* (www.cbmc.com) 2008
- David Murrow, *Men's League* (**http://mensleague.org/**)
- Steve Sonderman, *Top Gun Ministries* (Elmbrook Church 800-919-9059 www.topgunministries.org)

Bible Studies
- Brad Stewart, *Becoming a Kingdom Warrior*, (**www.kingdomwarrior.net/MMTools.htm**
- Brad Stewart, A Man After God's Heart (Charleston, SC: CreateSpace Publishing)
- Brad Stewart, A Man After God's Righteousness, (Charleston, SC: CreateSpace Publishing)
- Brad Stewart, A Man After God's Reward, (Charleston, SC: CreateSpace Publishing)
- Gene Getz, *Joshua – Living as a Consistent Role Model* (Nashville, TN: B&H Publishing Group, 1995)
- Gene Getz, *David – Seeking God Faithfully* (Nashville, TN: B&H Publishing Group, 1995)
- Gene Getz, *Joseph – Overcoming Obstacles Through Faithfulness* (Nashville, TN: B&H Publishing Group, 1996)
- Gene Getz, *Moses – Freeing Yourself to Know God* (Nashville, TN: B&H Publishing Group, 1997)
- Gene Getz, *Paul – Living for the Call of Christ* (Nashville, TN: B&H Publishing Group, 2000)
- Gene Getz, *Samuel – A Lifetime of Serving* (Nashville, TN: B&H Publishing Group, 1997)
- Lifeguide Bible Studies – (InterVarsity Press)
- Life Change Bible Studies – (NavPress)

Rite of Passage
- Chuck Stecker, *Men of Honor, Women of Virtue* (Colorado Springs, CO: Cook Communications, 2006)

Appendix D – Troubleshooting Unique Men's Ministry Situations

Why should my church start a men's ministry?

When it comes to troubles in the world, life is warfare, and "There ain't no rear to this battle nowhere!" When it comes to living, men cannot run away and hide. Crime rates continue to rise. Abortion is a method of birth control. Homosexuality is an alternate life style. Adultery is a common event. Kidnapping and molestations are weekly news. Besides these horrific behaviors, each year more men, women, and children contract AIDS. Men are living without moral direction, and the results are devastating to society. The more men live without moral direction, the deeper our moral decadence. As the decadence deepens, the battle bulges.

Even in the church men today are in crisis. They are confused over what it means and does not mean to be a man. Thus, confused men cause many problems. Here are four reasons why men struggle:

❧ *Friendless* – Most men over the age of thirty-five do not have one close friend they could call in the middle of the night.

❧ *Sexually Addicted* – With the internet making these addictions private, Christian men are spending time in front of their computer staring at images of naked women and sexually performances. Some addiction ministry experts' estimate addicted church men at 60%.

❧ *Emotionally Isolated* – Men struggle with identifying and expressing their emotions in a healthy manner. Most men express their emotion through acting in anger.

❧ *Spiritually Empty* – Men are unable to make sense of the world they live or the problems they face. Men need a safe place they can go where they are heard, understood, and taken seriously.

Unfortunately, the average church continues to see attendance drop. Since 1991, Barna's surveys point out church attendance, Bible reading, Sunday school attendance, volunteering at church, and giving to a church have all decreased for men but increased for women. Within the context of a life giving men's ministry for men, someone struggling with any of these needs will have the opportunity too to share his struggles, concerns, dreams, and victories. A team of men can band together in a masculine context to provide one another with encouragement and support as they work to live as intentional followers of Jesus Christ. When men start to relate to each other with godly trust, authenticity, and honesty, real transformation takes place. A life-giving men's ministry is a place where men learn the basics and apply them as they walk with Jesus.

Jesus was a different type of rabbi who demonstrated care and concern for women and children, but He built the foundation of His church by investing heavily in twelve men. Unfortunately, most local churches reverse this approach by allocating much more money and manpower for children's ministry, youth ministry, college ministry, singles ministry, women's ministry, even nursery ministry before resources are invested in men's ministry.

Men's ministry was the primary ministry of Jesus. In fact, the earthly ministry of Jesus was almost exclusively to a band of men who became a band of brothers. Through His life style and teaching, Jesus demonstrated to His men what they were supposed to do and how they were supposed to do it. Jesus focused on making disciples of men and then turned them into disciple makers.

AB Bruce in his classic Training of the Twelve provides this comment on the early ministry of Jesus,

> "That these calls were given with conscious reference to an ulterior end, even the apostleship, appears from the remarkable terms in which the earliest of them was expressed. "Follow Me," said Jesus to the fishermen of Bethsaida, "and I will make you fishers of men." These words (whose originality stamps them as a genuine saying of Jesus) show that the great Founder of the faith desired not only to have disciples, but to have about Him men whom He might train to make disciples of others: to cast the net of divine truth into the sea of the world, and to land on the shores of the divine kingdom a great multitude of believing souls. Both from His words and from His actions we can see that He attached supreme importance to that part of His work which consisted in training the twelve.

Christ Jesus is the foundation of the church, but he called men to be the backbone. Unfortunately, we see a lot of local churches with women leading in the void left by a visible absence of men. The first thing Christ did was to gather men for ministry. If more men were living as disciples more children would receive instruction from the father rather than from the mother, youth pastor, or Sunday school teacher. Although children often benefit from receiving spiritual instruction outside the home, the responsibility always remains with the father.

Starting and growing a vibrant ministry to and through men adds vitality to the church, builds godly leaders, and adds valuable resources to the body. Men who receive discipleship training are more apt to live as committed disciple of Christ, give more of their time, their talents, and their treasure.

Does your local place of worship have enough male leaders serving the body by leading in the home, helping on Sunday morning, glorifying God on the job, or discipling the next generation?

When you reach the man you impact the home. When you impact the home you change the local church. When you change the local church you transform the community. When you transform the community you change the world.

Why is it so difficult to get men to attend a men's ministry event?

Most pastors and men's ministry leaders agree that me are the hardest group to motivate to attend a local or regional men's ministry event. Gary Yagel, a PCA pastor, has posted six unique characteristics of men in response to this question.[v]

- Nearly all of the subgroups in the church (children, teens, college kids, singles, women, seniors) are strongly motivated to come to church events because they want to be with their friends. Men are not. Therefore, they don't show up just because the bulletin says that a men's event is planned.

- Your men's event takes men away from their homes. Many men already feel guilty about being away from home so much to do their jobs.

- For the 21st century man, time is the commodity of highest value. There has been an explosion of activities to compete for his time, from Karate for his kids to 200 channels on TV, including sports channels that have games nearly twenty-four hours a day. The length of the American work day is the highest it has ever been, while commuting time is increasing. He has less free time to give to a men's event than ever before.

- Today's men are tired and busy. They spend their days in the work world where products and activities are assigned a bottom-line value. That is the way they will see your men's event. Is the value of the event worth the time and effort to be involved? Out of a sense of commitment to the church, a man may come once to a men's event. But tired, busy men will not consistently attend something that does not have high value to them.

- The availability of graphic pornography at the click of a mouse means that more men are enslaved to secret sins than ever before. They may participate in something safe like playing softball. But, they won't come regularly to events that get them connected to other men at the spiritual level. On the one hand, they know they need help, but they are terrified of the shame they would experience if they were found out.

- Because of the way God has hardwired men, they are much more likely to come to an event when personally invited by another man. Most churches have not built a strong men's ministry leadership team that reaches out to the men of the congregation to make these personal invitations. Instead, they resort to bulletin or pulpit announcements which are not very effective.

Although men are tough to mobilize it can happen and will if men's ministry leaders apply a few simple practices and deliver some quality materials. Have a plan (see section on Mobilizing Men to a Men's Ministry Event) and a goal in mind. Kingdom Warrior recommends providing every man the necessary five to seven points of contact needed for him to make an informed decision to attend an event.

Why is there a loss of momentum after a men's ministry event?

Too many men's ministries start out well yet finish poorly. Part of the reason for this has to do with understanding the nature of men. Most men look at life in steps. Leaders will do much better at keeping momentum when they provide multiple entry points with various levels of commitment. The success of each entry point is maximized when it fits into an overall strategy that meets the needs of men and moves them down the path of increased commitment and Bible knowledge.

Effective men's ministries strategically organize different types of gatherings that work together as a whole. The funnel model illustrates how they fit with each other. There are six distinct types of entry points for men: special events, men's conferences, training seminars, congregational meetings, small group meetings, and man-to-man sessions.

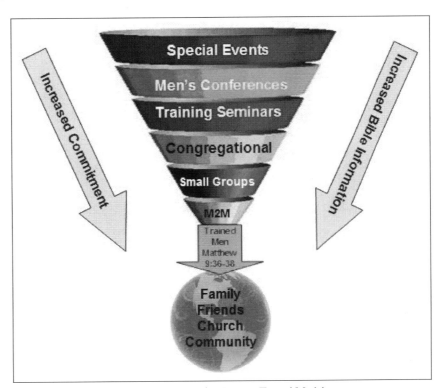

Figure 11 - Men's Ministry Funnel Model

When your men's ministry provides a variety of entry points, you make it easier for men to get involved. The men in your church are in different seasons of life and have different interests. How much they get involved will depend on their interest in spiritual things, their readiness, and the time they have available.

Another important consideration is the goal for your entry points. Each point should provide an opportunity for men to grow in their relationships with other men. Some events will seem more appealing than others. One big thing you want to avoid is appearing boring and irrelevant. Over and over men's surveys rank this as one of the biggest reasons why men dislike going to church.

Create momentum by creating value. When you create value with an activity you create momentum. Like a gear that makes a wheel turn, so do's momentum to your ministry. Capture Momentum by providing the right next step. Don't create momentum without a plan for how you will capture it. Make the follow-up fit the event, right size the commitment you are asking for, have an ending point, and help men take the next step. NOTE: if you consistently fail to capture momentum when you create it, you will not build a sustainable ministry. *Always show men a next right step.* Sustain momentum through relationships. Together, they can become authentic disciples who can transform the world around them.

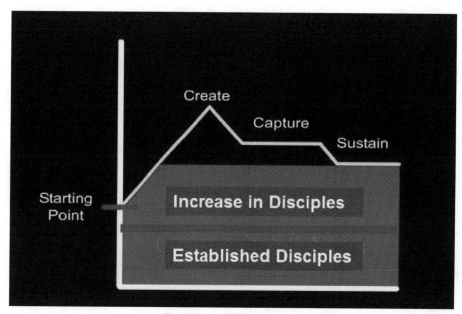

Figure 12 - Momentum Cycle

It is a normal cycle for numbers to drop off after an event. They key to growing your ministry is to increase your net margin of disciples. Generally speaking the first two layers of the funnel help create momentum, the second two help capture momentum, and the last two sustain momentum.

As a funnel provides a narrowing parameter for pouring liquid into a container, so the funnel demonstrates the progression of a man's involvement in the local church. For successful progression men must understand the need for increased commitment and biblical information. The left side of the funnel represents an increased commitment; the right side of the funnel represents increased biblical information. As the events progress down the funnel, they require a greater degree of commitment and they impart a greater degree of biblical information. The main goal of an effective ministry to and through its men, is to help them transfer biblical truth into every day application as they lead their families, grow in friendships, impact their churches, and change their communities. In the end they become laborers in the harvest fields of the earth (Matthew 9:36-39).

Why is church attendance decreasing for men but increasing for women?

According to Barna women are shouldering most of the responsibility for the health and vitality of the Christian faith in the country. He further asserts that without women, Christianity would have nearly 60% fewer adherents. The survey data show that nearly half of the nation's women have beliefs which classify them as born again (46%), compared to just about one-third of men (36%). In other words, there are between 11 million and 13 million more born again women than there are born again men in the country. Christianity is still the "faith-of-choice" among Americans, but particularly among women. When asked to identify their religious affiliation, 9 out of every 10 women nationwide (90%) said that they consider themselves to be Christian (compared to 83% of men).vi

Author David Murrow states, "Like a glove that gradually conforms to the hand of its wearer, Christianity has, over the centuries, subtly conformed to the needs and expectations of its most faithful constituency, women age 40 and older. So instead taking up the epic struggle Jesus promised his disciples, today's congregations focus on creating a warm, nurturing environment where the top priority is making everyone feel loved and accepted. We gather. We worship. We love each other. We sing. We instruct children. We comfort the hurting. This lineup is both beneficial and biblical, but these things alone will not galvanize men."vii

Pastors and men's ministry leaders must face the fact that attendance is decreasing for men and increasing for women. Kingdom Warrior advocates taking some time to change what may be considered more effeminate church service to a service that is considered a bit more masculine, or at a minimum to balance the service with aspects that would appeal to both men and women. For more information on this subject see the section Creating a Masculine Context in the Local Church.

One excellent resource for helping reach more men is to host a Go for the Guys Sunday. To learn more of this type of event visit http://www.churchformen.com/leaders.php

Why is our men's ministry program not working?

There could be several reasons why a men's ministry program is not working. If the leadership team is not aware of them they can slow down and eventually stop the work you are attempting to accomplish. Below are eight potential problems and a brief description.

- *Lack of pastoral support.* Men need to know that the senior pastor is 100% behind the ministry to men. This does not mean he has to run the day-to-day operation. Only that he has a visible presence and audible support. Men must honor and respect their pastor by seeking his counsel and release on any men's ministry activities. Your pastor's prayers, presence and promotion are essential to a successful men's ministry in your church - he "sets the pace" as a leader. Ministries actively supported by the senior pastor grow at a much faster rate and the men live much healthier lives.

- *Focus on programs and events, not on relationships.* When a ministry is based on events and activities, it does not take long for men to stop participating. They have been there, done that, got the T shirt, coffee cup, and the pen. Men's ministry based on relationships is a much better model. Most men attend because of the relationships they are developing.

- *Mix men and women.* It is a known fact the depth of sharing openly and honestly with women present is almost non-existent for men. If you are going to have a mixed event, do not make it a men's ministry event.

- *Lack sufficient entry points.* Early in the ministry process you will have fewer entry points than a ministry that has been up and running for three to five years. This is normal. However, if after several years you are still operating with one or two, the lack of sufficient entry points will retard your growth.

- *Lack clear goals and direction.* Men like to know where you are taking them, there is a good plan in place, and that the event has value to them. Be sure to let the men know the relationships between the events. For example, how does your Saturday breakfast relate to the small groups, the small groups relate to the monthly service project. Every entry point should promote relationships; have relevance, and a return on your churches investment.

- *Too rigid with no flexibility.* Sooner or later you will experience scheduling conflicts, men failing to complete an assigned task, or nature interfering with your well designed plans. Stay flexible and look for the lesson God wants to teach you. It may well be He has an alternate plan that is much better than your original. Or it may be that you have a lesson to learn in the given situation.

- *Try to implement too much too fast.* This is one of the most common pitfalls of an early ministry to men. A solid well tuned ministry to and through men takes three to five years to build. Be patient and plan for the long haul. Otherwise you can spread yourself to thin, reach burnout, and lose focus on the primary reason for your ministry.

✟ *Led by one man.* This is another pretty common problem. While it is important to have a men's ministry champion, it is critical to have a leadership team in place to share the work and continue with equipping men for works of service. A men's leadership team is the heart of an effective men's ministry in your church as they pray, direct, and administer the entire men's ministry. This is critical to sustain the work if someone moves or changes ministries.

What are the biggest spiritual needs for men in the local church?

Kingdom Warrior has found the following items are the top ten issues for men in the local church. Pastors and men's ministry leaders will do well to have a systematic focus on each item while keeping in mind the importance of helping them become mature disciples. Mature disciples intentionally live to serve the King and reproduce a kingdom life in others.

✟ *Relationship with God* – Most Christian men have a basic understanding of Christ but do not understand that having a personal relationship with Jesus begins when they repent from their sin and lasts for eternity. Godly men disciples produce lasting fruit.

✟ *Sexuality and Lust* – Some church experts estimate at least 60% of all church men are routinely spending time viewing pornography on the internet. Sex, lust, purity, and pornography are all issues men need help dealing with on a daily basis.

✟ *Anger* – Most men struggle with losing their temper and being impatient with others. God's men need to know how to process anger without going into rage.

✟ *Marriage* – This is one of the leading issues men need help with. Too many homes are being destroyed by divorce and so called "healthy separations." It is critical for men to learn what it means to love their wives as Christ loved the church.

✟ *Family Leadership in the Home* – Too many husbands and fathers act one way in the church or at work and another when they are at church. According to the National Coalition for Men's ministries out of every ten men in the average church nine will have children who leave the church.

✟ *Personal Management* – The older a man gets the more life seems to demand of his time and energy. Men need to know how to manage life by focusing on the right priorities and Christian disciplines.

✟ *Career* – Men must learn to work to the glory of God as well as understand the difference between success and significance. They need to see their job as a calling from God where they apply practical Biblical wisdom.

↘ *Friendship and Accountability* – Most American males over the age of 35 do not have a close friend. The church should be a place where men can develop life long friendships that have the potential to be like Jonathan and David.

↘ *Outreach* – For the church to grow men must learn the importance of sharing their faith and seeking the lost. Men are looking for a challenging place where they labor and conquer. Provide them with an outreach plan where they can win men, women, and children to Christ.

↘ *Integrity* – Men need to know God's standard for morality, ethics, and godly character so they can live by godly principles and not by worldly circumstances.

Why should I survey my men?

This may seem pretty clear to some readers; however, a lot of leaders do not take a climate survey of the men. Surveys provide pastors and men's ministry with demographics and data that help determine which areas to focus or more important they give you the true pulse of your men and help you to see their strengths and weaknesses. Confidential surveys work and work well when applied to your battle plans for the future.

Without taking an anonymous survey of all your men, you put yourself in a position of having to guess what the men want and need. Furthermore, many men will not share openly or clearly what their needs are. Leaders often miss the mark of clearly identifying men's needs and therefore launch a ministry based on false assumptions. This has been the cause of many men's ministry failures.

Several survey options are available to a Kingdom Warrior church client. Some pastors and leaders prefer to use on-line versions while others prefer a paper based system. This section gives you helpful tools for both options.

On-line Survey Tool

On-line versions provide users with quick and easy access to the survey questions as well as ensure all the questions are answered before the survey is considered complete. Users can access the system from any computer with internet access and web browser. The system is convenient and private. The weakness for this system is getting men to trust it is private and to take the time to sit at a computer and fill out the survey.

Kingdom Warrior recommends using a free system offered by Iron Sharpens Iron. You can find more information about this service at www.ironsharpensiron.net/survey.php

This is how their system works:

1. Sign-up for the survey. There is no fee but we encourage you to generously give to the regional ministry in your area that is hosting an Iron Sharpens Iron Conference.

2. We will add your church name and city to the drop down menu at the first page of the survey. Your men will choose your church from this menu.

3. We will send a link to the online survey to the contact person's email from the survey sign-up sheet.

4. The survey will be live and available to your men for 30 days 24x7.

5. At the end of the survey period, the contact person will receive an email with results and analysis.

Paper Based Survey Tool

The paper based survey tool provides users with a survey that is easy to customize. Kingdom Warrior recommends using a survey that collects data using six key areas: Demographics, Personal Development, Identity with Christ, Issues Facing Men, Ministry Activities and Men's Conferences. There are thirty questions broken into six distinct areas plus a place for additional comments. This survey contains thirty line items each one in soft copy that can be altered to suit your needs. Print the survey out one side only. If you do two sided, there is a good possibility your men will not fill the back sides.

Pros for this tool include customization for local church needs, quick single point distribution, and short turn around collection. Cons are the length and need for privacy while filling them out. Some men sitting next to a spouse or other men may not feel the freedom to be candid with all of their answers.

After your men complete this survey you will have a better understanding of their

- Demographics
- Personal Development
- Identity with Christ
- Issues Facing Men
- Ministry Activities
- Men's Conferences
- Additional Comments

In addition to the soft copy of the survey is a spread sheet for you to calculate the results. Use this as a basis for planning and justifying your plan for ministry.

Your survey should be distributed to as many of your men as possible. Some leaders opt to use mass distribution on Sunday morning and then have men drop the completed survey into a box.

As the internet and handheld technology continues to grow, so will the need for churches and ministries to leverage new tools. Be sure to check with our web site for the latest developments regarding surveys, automatic texts, mpegs, and downloads for ministry.

Below are two surveys, one for leaders and one for all the men. The leader survey evaluates the functions of an existing team while the general survey evaluates the needs of men. After the general survey is a corresponding score sheet. Both documents can be easily modified to fit the needs of a local church.

Appendix E – Surveys and Score Sheets

Men's Ministry Leadership Survey

Check the statements below that best describe your men's ministry.

1. Purpose Statement

☐ 1.1 We do not have a purpose statement/slogan for men's ministry.
☐ 1.2 We have a stated but unwritten purpose statement/slogan.
☐ 1.3 We have activities but not a ministry focus
☐ 1.4 We have a developed purpose statement /slogan with ministry-focused activities

2. Leadership

☐ 2.1 We do not have an identified men's ministry leadership team.
☐ 2.2 We have one or two men who provide leadership to our men's ministry.
☐ 2.3 We have developed a broad-based leadership team.

3. Study Groups

☐ 3.1 We currently do not have men meeting in study groups.
☐ 3.2 We have several study groups that are meeting regularly.
☐ 3.3 We have many study groups that are meeting regularly.

4. Relationships

☐ 4.1 We do not have accountability relationships developed among the men in our church.
☐ 4.2 We have sporadic development of relationships among men; there is little accountability.
☐ 4.3 We have seen strong, vital relationships develop among men in the church; there is high accountability.

5. Scheduled Activities

☐ 5.1 We have one or two men's ministry activities a year.
☐ 5.2 We have some regularly scheduled men's ministry activities each year.
☐ 5.3 We have planned men's ministry activities to encourage men to participate at various levels of interest.

6. Outreach

☐ 6.1 We are seeing little or no participation in our men's ministry.
☐ 6.2 We are seeing some involvement in our men's ministry.
☐ 6.3 We have a large number of men who are involved in our men's ministry and they are actively inviting others.

7. Impact on the Family

☐ 7.1 We have a few men leading some form of regular family devotions in their home.
☐ 7.2 We have many men who lead some form of regular family devotions in their home.
☐ 7.3 We have men helping other men lead some form of regular family devotions in their home.

8. Impact on the Church

☐ 8.1 We have a few men who are active and who are having an impact in the church.
☐ 8.2 We have a core group of men who are committed to the pastor and the ministry of the church.
☐ 8.3 We have a significant number of men actively supporting the pastor and involved in church ministry.[viii]

9. Atmosphere at the Church

☐ 9.1 We have a church atmosphere that emphasizes loving God, building caring relationships, and healing from wounds.
☐ 9.2 We have a church atmosphere that promotes a male friendly environment, which loves God and builds caring relationships.
☐ 9.3 We have a church atmosphere that balances a male friendly environment with a female friendly environment.
☐ 9.4 We have a church atmosphere that uses masculine language in challenging men to follow Christ and walk with God.

Men's Ministry Climate Survey

Hello Men. In order for [Church Name] to develop a first class ministry for all our men, we need to have honest and candid feedback. Please read and respond to this simple three page questionnaire by completing all thirty questions. Your participation will make a difference in the lives of men.

Demographics

1. Age ☐13-19 ☐20-29 ☐30-39 ☐40-49 ☐50-59 ☐60 +

2. Marriage
   ☐ Never been married
   ☐ Was married and am now divorced
   ☐ Am presently married – first marriage
   ☐ Am presently married – married more than once

3. Children
   ☐ Presently have children living at home under age 13
   ☐ Presently have children living at home between 13 and 18
   ☐ Presently have children, who are living away from home
   ☐ Presently have no children

4. Work week? ☐<40hrs ☐40-45hrs ☐46-50hrs ☐51-55hrs ☐56-60hrs ☐>60

Personal Development

5. How long at your present job ☐< 1 yr ☐2-3 yrs ☐3-5 yrs ☐6-10 yrs ☐> 10 yrs

6. How would you measure your job satisfaction the past twelve months?
   ☐ Best year ever in my work life
   ☐ Very satisfying
   ☐ Satisfying
   ☐ Less than satisfying
   ☐ Anxious to move to different employment

7. How long as a Christian? ☐< 1 yr ☐2-3 yrs ☐3-5 yrs ☐6-10 yrs ☐> 10 yrs

8. How would you measure your growth in Christ the last twelve months?
   ☐ Most growth ever in my life in Christ
   ☐ Solid growth – not standing still
   ☐ Standing still – no measurable growth
   ☐ Struggling to grow for a variety of reasons

☐ Doing very poorly and need help

9. Do you have another man who helps you keep accountable in your walk with Christ?
☐ Yes ☐ No

Identify with Christ

10. How often have you invited another man to join you for Sunday morning worship at your church during the past two years?
☐ Weekly ☐ Monthly ☐ 2-3 times/yr ☐ Almost never ☐ Never

11. How often have you shared the Gospel message with another person during the past two years?
☐ Weekly ☐ Monthly ☐ 2-3 times/yr ☐ Almost never ☐ Never

12. If you are married, how often have you invited your wife to pray with you during the last two years (Do not include thanksgiving for meals)?
☐ Weekly ☐ Monthly ☐ 2-3 times/yr ☐ Almost never ☐ Never

13. If you have children at home, how often in the past two years have you purposely gathered the family together for Bible reading and prayer?
☐ Weekly ☐ Monthly ☐ 2-3 times/yr ☐ Almost never ☐ Never

Issues Facing Men

14. How often do you come into contact with pornography?
☐ Daily ☐ 2-3 Week ☐ Weekly ☐ Monthly ☐ 2-3 times/yr ☐ Never

15. How often do you loose your temper?
☐ Daily ☐ 2-3 Week ☐ Weekly ☐ Monthly ☐ 2-3 times/yr ☐ Never

16. How often do you gamble (Lottery, casino, on-line)?
☐ Daily ☐ 2-3 Week ☐ Weekly ☐ Monthly ☐ 2-3 times/yr ☐ Never

17. How often do you consume alcohol?
☐ Daily ☐ 2-3 Week ☐ Weekly ☐ Monthly ☐ 2-3 times/yr ☐ Never

18. How much alcohol do you consume (One drink is defined as 12 ounces of beer, 5 ounces of wine, or one standard cocktail (1.5 ounces of 80-proof liquor)?
☐ Never ☐ 1 monthly ☐ 2-4 monthly ☐ 2-4 weekly ☐ >5 weekly

19. How many drinks containing alcohol do you have on a typical day when you are drinking?
☐ 1 ☐ 1-2 ☐ 3-4 ☐ 5-6 ☐ >6

Ministry

20. What kind of Christian small group are you presently involved with (Check all that relate)?

☐ Not in a regular small group of any kind
☐ Once a month small group
☐ Weekly or bi-weekly group of men and women
☐ Weekly or bi-weekly group of men

21. Are you more likely to:

☐ Read a Christian book
☐ Listen to a Christian CD
☐ Listen to Christian radio
☐ Watch a Christian video
☐ Watch Christian television
☐ Watch non-Christian videos
☐ Watch non-Christian television
☐ I do none of the above

22. Please rate your interest in the items below: 1 = lowest through 6 = highest (mark one for each item)

a. Men's Bible Study	1	2	3	4	5	6
c. Camping trip	1	2	3	4	5	6
e. Golf scramble	1	2	3	4	5	6
g. Monthly breakfast	1	2	3	4	5	6
i. Chili cook-off	1	2	3	4	5	6
l. Men Sunday school	1	2	3	4	5	6
b. Sporting event	1	2	3	4	5	6
d. Fishing trip	1	2	3	4	5	6
f. Annual retreat	1	2	3	4	5	6
h. Service project	1	2	3	4	5	6
k. Father child outing	1	2	3	4	5	6
m. Equipping seminar	1	2	3	4	5	6

Low ------------------------- High

23. If you were to attend a seminar for men in the coming months, which ones would be of interest to you? Please check the top three.

☐ Furthering my Career   ☐ Developing Friendship with wife
☐ Godly Fathering   ☐ Deepening my Marriage
☐ Lust/Sexual Temptation   ☐ Becoming a Great Dad
☐ Witnessing   ☐ Managing money/Budgets
☐ Discipleship/Spiritual Growth ☐ Dealing with Anger
☐ Rites of Passage Training   ☐ Other

24. What level of interest do you have in participating in a book study where you read a book and then meet once a month to connect with men and comment on what you learned?

☐Not interested ☐A little interest ☐Somewhat interested ☐Very interested

Men's Conferences

25. What level of interest do you have in going with the men of [Church Name] to attend a one day conference?

☐Not interested ☐A little interest ☐Somewhat interested ☐Very interested

26. How much are you willing to pay for an all day Saturday conference?

☐$20.00 ☐$40.00 ☐$60.00 ☐$80.00 ☐$100.00

27. What level of interest do you have in going with the men of [Church Name] to attend an overnight conference leaving Friday and returning late Saturday night?

☐Not interested ☐A little interest ☐Somewhat interested ☐Very interested

28. How much are you willing to pay for an overnight conference (return home Saturday night)?
☐$40.00 ☐$60.00 ☐$80.00 ☐$100.00 ☐$120.00

29. What level of interest do you have in going with the men of [Church Name] to attend a full weekend conference leaving Friday and returning home Sunday afternoon?

☐Not interested ☐A little interest ☐Somewhat interested ☐Very interested

30. How much are you willing to pay for a full weekend (Friday – Sunday) overnight conference?

☐$80.00 ☐$100.00 ☐$120.00 ☐$140.00 ☐>$160.00

Comments

Thank you for taking the time to help us collect this information. Please share any comments you have on [Name of Men's Ministry] here at [Church Name]

Sample Score Sheet

Demographics									
1. Age		13-19	20-29	30-39	40-49	50-59	60+		
	Totals	1	0	0	0	0	0		
	%	100.00%	0.00%	0.00%	0.00%	0.00%	0.00%		
		Totals	%						
2. Marriage		1	100.00%	Never been married					
		0	0.00%	Was married and am now divorced					
		0	0.00%	Am presently married – first marriage					
		0	0.00%	Am presently married – married more than once					
		Totals	%						
3. Children		1	100.00%	Presently have children living at home under age 13					
		0	0.00%	Presently have children living at home between 13 and 18					
		0	0.00%	Presently have children, who are all living away from home					
		0	0.00%	Presently have no children					
4. How long is your work week? <40hrs 40-45hrs 46-50hrs 51-55hrs 56-60hrs >60									
			<40 hrs	40-45 hrs	45-50 hrs	51-55hrs	55-60 hrs	>60	
		Totals	1	0	0	0	0	0	
		%	100.00%	0.00%	0.00%	0.00%	0.00%	0.00%	

Personal Development

5. How long have you been at your present job

	< 1 yr	2-3 yrs	3-5yrs	6-10 yrs	> 10 yrs
Totals	1	0	0	0	0
%	100.00%	0.00%	0.00%	0.00%	0.00%

6. How would you measure your job satisfaction the past twelve months?

Totals	%	
1	100.00%	Best year ever in my work life
0	0.00%	Very satisfying
0	0.00%	Satisfying
0	0.00%	Less than satisfying
0	0.00%	Anxious to move to different employment

7. How long have you been a Christian?

	< 1 yr	2-3 yrs	3-5yrs	6-10 yrs	> 10 yrs
Totals	1	0	0	0	0
%	100.00%	0.00%	0.00%	0.00%	0.00%

8. How would you measure your growth in Christ the last twelve months?

Totals	%	
1	100.00%	Most growth ever in my life in Christ
0	0.00%	Solid growth – not standing still
0	0.00%	Standing still – no measurable growth
0	0.00%	Struggling to grow for a variety of reasons
0	0.00%	Doing very poorly and need help

9. Do you have another man who helps you keep accountable in your walk with Christ?

Totals	%	
1	100.00%	Yes
0	0.00%	No

Identify with Christ

10. How often have you invited another man to join you for Sunday morning worship at your church during the past two years?

	Weekly	Monthly	2-3 x yr	Alm Never	Never
Totals	1	0	0	0	0
%	100.00%	0.00%	0.00%	0.00%	0.00%

11. How often have you shared the Gospel message with another person during the past two years?

		Weekly	Monthly	2-3 x yr	Alm Never	Never
	Totals	1	0	0	0	0
	%	100.00%	0.00%	0.00%	0.00%	0.00%

12. If you are married, how often have you invited your wife to pray with you during the last two years (Do not include thanksgiving for meals)?

		Weekly	Monthly	2-3 x yr	Alm Never	Never
	Totals	1	0	0	0	0
	%	100.00%	0.00%	0.00%	0.00%	0.00%

13. If you have children at home, how often in the past two years have you purposely gathered the family together for Bible reading and prayer?

		Weekly	Monthly	2-3 x yr	Alm Never	Never
	Totals	1	0	0	0	0
	%	100.00%	0.00%	0.00%	0.00%	0.00%

Issues Facing Men

14. How often do you come into contact with pornography?

		Daily	2-3 week	Weekly	Monthly	2-3 x yr	Never
	Totals	1	0	0	0	0	0
	%	100.00%	0.00%	0.00%	0.00%	0.00%	0.00%

15. How often do you loose your temper?

		Daily	2-3 week	Weekly	Monthly	2-3 x yr	Never
	Totals	1	0	0	0	0	0
	%	100.00%	0.00%	0.00%	0.00%	0.00%	0.00%

16. How often do you gamble (Lottery, casino, on-line)?

		Daily	2-3 week	Weekly	Monthly	2-3 x yr	Never
	Totals	1	0	0	0	0	0
	%	100.00%	0.00%	0.00%	0.00%	0.00%	0.00%

17. How often to you consume alcohol?

		Daily	2-3 week	Weekly	Monthly	2-3 x yr	Never
	Totals	1	0	0	0	0	0

Daily 2-3 Week Weekly Monthly 2-3 times/yr Never	%	100.00 %	0.00%	0.00%	0.00%	0.00%	0.00%	

18. How much alcohol do you consume (One drink is defined as 12 ounces of beer, 5 ounces of wine, or one standard cocktail (1.5 ounces of 80-proof liquor)?

		Never	Monthly	2-4 x M	2-4 x Wk	>5 Weekly	
	Totals	1	0	0	0	0	
	%	100.00 %	0.00%	0.00%	0.00%	0.00%	

19. How many drinks containing alcohol do you have on a typical day when you are drinking?

		1	2-Jan	4-Mar	6-May	>6	
	Totals	1	0	0	0	0	
	%	100.00 %	0.00%	0.00%	0.00%	0.00%	

Ministry

20. What kind of Christian small group are you presently involved with (Check all that relate)?

	Totals	%				
	1	100.00 %	Not in a regular small group of any kind			
	0	0.00%	Once a month small group			
	0	0.00%	Weekly or bi-weekly group of men and women			
	0	0.00%	Weekly or bi-weekly group of men			

21. Are you more likely to:

	Totals	%				
	1	100.00 %	Read a Christian book			
	0	0.00%	Listen to a Christian CD			
	0	0.00%	Listen to Christian radio			
	0	0.00%	Watch a Christian video			
	0	0.00%	Watch Christian television			

22. Please rate your interest in the items below: 1 = low through 6 = highest (mark one for each item)

Score		1	2	3	4	5	6	
a. Men's Bible Study		1	0	0	0	0	0	
	%	100.00 %	0.00%	0.00%	0.00%	0.00%	0.00%	
c. Camping trip		1	0	0	0	0	0	
	%	100.00 %	0.00%	0.00%	0.00%	0.00%	0.00%	
e. Golf scramble		1	0	0	0	0	0	
	%	100.00	0.00%	0.00%	0.00%	0.00%	0.00%	

		%					
g. Monthly breakfast		1	0	0	0	0	0
	%	100.00%	0.00%	0.00%	0.00%	0.00%	0.00%
i. Chili cook-off		1	0	0	0	0	0
	%	100.00%	0.00%	0.00%	0.00%	0.00%	0.00%
l. Men Sunday school		1	0	0	0	0	0
	%	100.00%	0.00%	0.00%	0.00%	0.00%	0.00%
b. Sporting event		1	0	0	0	0	0
	%	100.00%	0.00%	0.00%	0.00%	0.00%	0.00%
d. Fishing trip		1	0	0	0	0	0
	%	100.00%	0.00%	0.00%	0.00%	0.00%	0.00%
f. Annual retreat		1	0	0	0	0	0
	%	100.00%	0.00%	0.00%	0.00%	0.00%	0.00%
h. Service project		1	0	0	0	0	0
	%	100.00%	0.00%	0.00%	0.00%	0.00%	0.00%
k. Father child outing		1	0	0	0	0	0
	%	100.00%	0.00%	0.00%	0.00%	0.00%	0.00%
m. Equipping seminar		1	0	0	0	0	0
	%	100.00%	0.00%	0.00%	0.00%	0.00%	0.00%

23. If you were to attend a seminar for men in the coming months, which ones would be of interest to you? Please check the top three.

	Totals	%	
	1	100.00%	Furthering my Career
	0	0.00%	Godly Fathering
	0	0.00%	Lust/Sexual Temptation
	0	0.00%	Time Management
	0	0.00%	Rites of Passage Training
	0	0.00%	Discipleship/Spiritual Growth
	0	0.00%	Developing a Friendship with my wife
	0	0.00%	Deepening my Marriage
	0	0.00%	Becoming a Great Dad
	0	0.00%	Managing money/Budgets
	0	0.00%	Dealing with Anger
	0	0.00%	Other _____

24. What level of interest do you have in participating in a book study where you read a book and then meet once a month to connect with men and comment on what you learned?

		No interest	A little interset	Somwhat Interested	Very Interested
	Totals	1	0	0	0
	%	100.00	0.00%	0.00%	0.00%

		%					

Men's Conferences

25. What level of interest do you have in attending a one day conference?

		No interest	A little interset	Somwhat Interested	Very Interested
	Tot als	1	0	0	0
	%	100.00%	0.00%	0.00%	0.00%

26. How much are you willing to pay for an all day Saturday conference?

		$20.00	$40.00	$60.00	$80.00	$100.00		
	Totals	1	0	0	0	0		
	%	100.00%	0.00%	0.00%	0.00%	0.00%		

27. What level of interest do you have in attending an overnight conference leaving Friday and returning late Saturday night?

		No interest	A little interset	Somwhat Interested	Very Interested
	Tot als	1	0	0	0
	%	100.00%	0.00%	0.00%	0.00%

28. How much are you willing to pay for an overnight conference (return home Saturday night)?

		$20.00	$40.00	$60.00	$80.00	$100.00		
	Totals	1	0	0	0	0		
	%	100.00%	0.00%	0.00%	0.00%	0.00%		

29. What level of interest do you have in attending a weekend conference leaving Friday and returning home Sunday afternoon?

		No interest	A little interset	Somwhat Interested	Very Interested
	Tot als	1	0	0	0
	%	100.00%	0.00%	0.00%	0.00%

30. How much are you willing to pay for a full weekend (Friday – Sunday) overnight conference?

		$40.00	$60.00	$80.00	$100.00	>$120.00		
	Totals	1	0	0	0	0		
	%	100.00%	0.00%	0.00%	0.00%	0.00%		

Footnotes

[i] Dictionary (Naples, FL: Typhoon International Corp, 2003) pg 755

ii See NMLB ch 8

iii Patrick Morley, Pastoring Men (Chicago, IL: Moody Publishers) pg 88

iv http://www.barna.org/FlexPage.aspx?Page=BarnaUpdate&BarnaUpdateID=47

v http://www.pcacep.org/Men/faq.htm

vi http://www.barna.org/FlexPage.aspx?Page=BarnaUpdate&BarnaUpdateID=47

vii http://www.churchformen.com/leaders.php

viii Men's Ministry in the 21st Century (Loveland, CO. Group Publishing, 2004) pg . 86

Made in the USA
Columbia, SC
06 March 2023

13047928R00080